*Baptists and the
Emerging Church Movement*

Baptists and the Emerging Church Movement

A Baptistic Assessment of Four Themes of
Emerging Church Ecclesiology

David Mark Rathel

WIPF & STOCK · Eugene, Oregon

BAPTISTS AND THE EMERGING CHURCH MOVEMENT
A Baptistic Assessment of Four Themes of Emerging Church Ecclesiology

Copyright © 2014 David Mark Rathel. All rights reserved. Except for brief quotations in critical publications or reviews, no part of this book may be reproduced in any manner without prior written permission from the publisher. Write: Permissions. Wipf and Stock Publishers, 199 W. 8th Ave., Suite 3, Eugene, OR 97401.

Wipf and Stock
An Imprint of Wipf and Stock Publishers
199 W. 8th Ave., Suite 3
Eugene, OR 97401

www.wipfandstock.com

ISBN 13: 978-1-62564-493-0

Manufactured in the U.S.A.   07/29/2014

To April Rathel, a constant source of help and encouragement.

Contents

Acknowledgements | ix

Introduction | 1
1 Understanding the Emerging Church | 5
2 Assessing Emerging Church Community | 19
3 Assessing Emerging Church Worship and Preaching | 42
4 Assessing Emerging Church Missional Ministry | 67
5 Assessing Emerging Church Leadership | 95
Conclusion | 116

Bibliography | 119

Acknowledgments

THE SUPPORT OF A number of people has made this book possible. I wish to acknowledge them here and give them the honor they are due. First, I am tremendously grateful for my wife, April, who has served as a constant source of encouragement and support. Second, I am grateful to my church family, Fork Baptist Church, for graciously giving me the time necessary to complete this project. Third, I wish to recognize my mentoring professor, Dr. John Hammett, for offering helpful advice and creating in me an interest in Baptist ecclesiology. Finally, I wish to express gratitude to my parents, Mark and Angela Rathel, as well as my grandparents, Bob and Lovelle Wilkerson, for teaching me to love Christ.

Introduction

FOR THIS PROJECT, I will research four themes present in the ecclesiological proposals of popular leaders of the emerging church movement and evaluate them from a Baptistic understanding of the church. I will argue that though not all emerging church ecclesiology conflicts with Baptist thought, many of the proposals that originate from the more radical streams of the movement (e.g., revisionists and some reconstructionists) tend to stand in opposition to Baptist ecclesiology.

Emerging writers have not produced anything resembling a systematic theology, so organizing emerging thought in a structured way presents a difficult task. However, extensive reading of emerging church literature reveals that emerging writers typically focus on four key ecclesiological themes. I will therefore address these four themes, which emerging writers of all theological persuasions seem to emphasize: the church as a community, the worship/preaching ministry of the church, the church's missional engagement, and the church's leadership.[1]

Historic Baptist ecclesiology will form the plumb line for evaluating emerging church ecclesiology.[2] A Baptistic understanding of ecclesiology makes a profitable reference point for a number

---

1. These four central themes are similar to those discovered by John Hammett as detailed in Hammett, "Church according to Emergent/Emerging Church," 224–25.

2. I will draw from important Baptist confessions of faith in addition to well-known Baptist theologians who have written on ecclesiological issues.

of reasons. First, Baptists represent an important branch of historic Christianity. Second, Baptists have a well-noted history of thinking through ecclesiological issues and have made solid contributions to this field.[3] Third, many would affirm that a Baptistic understanding of the church represents an ecclesiological model that aligns closely with the New Testament's teachings.[4] By writing this Baptistic evaluation of emerging ecclesiology, I hope to give younger Baptists a tool by which they can critically evaluate the emerging church's ecclesiological proposals.

Chapter 1 will serve as an introductory chapter. In it, I will describe the origins of the emerging church movement and demonstrate that ecclesiology has been the movement's central concern since its inception. I will also introduce the aforementioned ecclesiological themes that surface in much emerging church literature. In the chapter's conclusion, I will seek to explain the relevance that discussions on emerging church ecclesiology have for Baptists today.

In chapter 2, I will survey and assess emerging church proposals intended to create an intimate church community. Traditionally, when speaking of the makeup of the church community, Baptists have emphasized the importance of maintaining a regenerate church body. They have historically employed three practices to maintain a regenerate church body: public professions of faith via believer's baptism, a clearly defined church membership, and shared church covenants and confessions of faith. I will therefore assess emerging church proposals related to church community in light of their potential impact upon these three historic practices. I

---

3. One can find a discussion on the ecclesiological contributions made by Baptists in Norman, *More than Just a Name*.

4. For example, R. Stanton Norman writes, "Baptists, along with other Christian denominations, appeal to the Bible as their ultimate or sole source for religious authority. Baptists distance themselves from other denominations, however, by claiming a complete dependence upon Scripture as the principle foundation for their beliefs and practices. Whereas certain other Christian groups incorporate extra-biblical sources such as tradition for religious authority, Baptists in their distinctive writings contend that they alone consistently and exclusively hold to the Bible exclusively as their religious authority." Norman, "Southern Baptist Identity," 44–45.

Introduction

will consider such emerging proposals as the belonging-before-belief model, the centered-set model, the structureless church model, the liquid church model, and emerging revisionists' understanding of love and toleration.

In chapter 3, I will survey and assess emerging church proposals related to public worship and preaching. Emerging leaders desire to create experiential and participatory worship gatherings. To accomplish this, they typically call for a return to ancient worship practices, such as labyrinths and prayer stations, and for a greater emphasis on the arts in worship. They also emphasize participation and experience during the preaching time, with Doug Pagitt going so far as to invite the congregation to participate in the construction of the sermon while the he delivers it.[5] While Baptists have allowed for diversity in worship styles, they have historically shared a desire to make Scripture the central focus of the worship gathering. I will assess emerging proposals related to worship and preaching in light of this strong focus on Scripture.

In chapter 4, I will survey and assess the emerging church's understanding of the term missional. Mark Driscoll uses the term missional to refer to the need for a local church to reach into its community, contextualize its message to its surrounding culture, and employ modern technologies to reach as large an audience as possible. In the name of being missional, Driscoll's church employs digital technology to connect multiple churches together in order to form one large church.[6]

---

5. Pagitt, *Preaching Re-Imagined*, 23.

6. The Mars Hill website states, "Though by definition we may be many different churches, the Mars Hill Network of churches remains a single, united church. We share a common infrastructure, a common mission, common teaching, and a common belief that we can reach more people by working together rather than existing separately." I will elaborate upon this in chapter 4. Originally at Mars Hill website, "No More Mars Hill 'Campuses,'" http://marshill.com/2011/08/08/no-more-mars-hill-campuses; that link is no longer working, but references to and quotes from that article can be found at Alex Murashko, "Mars Hill Church: Don't Call Us 'Campuses' Anymore," *Christian Post*, August 11, 2011, http://www.christianpost.com/news/mars-hill-church-dont-call-us-campuses-anymore-53736.

Other emerging leaders use the term missional to speak of the need for the church to emphasize social ministry. Such leaders believe that contemporary evangelicals miss the overarching message of Scripture by focusing singularly on personal conversion. Brian McLaren, for example, declares his opposition to the view that "life is about being (or getting) saved."[7] Instead, he argues that "salvation means being rescued from fruitless ways of life here and now, to share in God's saving love for all creation, in an adventure called the kingdom of God."[8] This so-called "broader" understanding of salvation plays a significant role in much emerging church literature with emerging leaders calling upon churches to restore their local communities through social work. Proposals related to the nature of the church (multiple churches considered to be one large church) and the mission of the church (the church as a performer of social ministry and community restoration) will obviously interest Baptists. I will assess these proposals in light of what Baptists have historically written on local church autonomy and the church's mission.

In chapter 5, I will survey and assess emerging church proposals related to church leadership. Some emerging church revisionists argue for the removal of any publicly recognized leadership within the church. They desire a leaderless group. On the opposite end of the emerging spectrum, relevants such as Dan Kimball and Mark Driscoll favor traditional church structures but attempt to practice them with sensitivity toward the concerns of postmoderns. Between these two positions rests Frost and Hirsch's APEPT model, an attempt to incorporate the teachings of Ephesians 4:11 into the church and its mission.[9] Focusing on such maters a congregational polity, the role of pastors, and Christ as the head of the church, I will assess these three proposals in light of what Baptists have historically believed in regards to church leadership.

---

7. McLaren and Campolo, *Adventures in Missing the Point*, 19.

8. Ibid.

9. The APEPT model is not unique to Frost and Hirsch or even to the emerging church movement. See, for example, Simson, *Houses That Change the World*, and Wagner, *Apostles and Prophets*.

1

Understanding the Emerging Church Movement

GARY GILLEY DESCRIBED THE difficulty in defining the emerging church movement when he wrote, "The movement is so new, so fragmented, so varied, that nailing it down is like nailing down the proverbial JELL-O to the wall."[1] Mark Liederbach and Alvin Reid echo Gilley's frustration when they write that defining the movement is "as difficult as trying to catch fish with one's bare hands. Just when you think you have a handle on it, the idea shifts and eludes your grasp."[2] Other writers have used adjectives such as chameleon-like, perplexingly amorphous, and ill-defined to describe the movement.[3]

The emerging church movement possesses three attributes that create such difficulties. First, the movement is primarily one of protest.[4] Standing in opposition to the traditional model of church,

1. Gilley, *This Little Church Stayed Home*, 142.
2. Liederbach and Reid, *Convergent Church*, 78–79.
3. James K. A. Smith uses the term chameleon to describe the movement in Smith, "Emerging Church," 40. Phil Johnson uses the phrase perplexingly amorphous in Johnson, "Joyriding on the Downgrade," 212. D. A. Carson accuses the movement of being ill-defined in Carson, *Becoming Conversant*, 14–15.
4. Many respected observers of the movement have noticed this protest

most emerging works have focused solely upon detailing what the emerging movement is against rather than describing what it supports.[5] Second, the movement is not fully developed, and emerging writers have not addressed many theological and methodological issues.[6] Third, a large degree of diversity exists within the movement. Phil Johnson has stated that the movement "has no clear homogeneity in doctrine, philosophy, or practice."[7] The fact that thinkers as diverse as Mark Driscoll and Brian McLaren have both been associated with the movement gives credence to Johnson's claim.

Researchers examining the emerging church movement must therefore exercise great caution in order to ensure that they describe and define the movement correctly. In this chapter, I will attempt to lay the foundation necessary for accurately assessing the emerging church from a Baptistic perspective. I will first trace the origins of the emerging church in order to place the movement's protest element within its proper historical context. Second, I will introduce one area that the leaders of this new movement have sufficiently probed, ecclesiology. Third, I will address the movement's diversity by categorizing the different streams of thought that exist among emerging church leaders. I will conclude the chapter by explaining why the emerging church discussion is relevant for contemporary theologians, particularly those from the Baptist tradition.

---

element. For example, Jim Belcher writes, "It doesn't take long in reading the literature of the emerging church to realize that protest is at the heart of their teaching." See Belcher, *Deep Church*, 38. See also Mark Devine, who uses the theme of protest as a key descriptor of movement. Devine, "Emerging Church," 4–46.

5. For example, Gibbs and Bolger, two respected researchers on the emerging church, have written, "Emerging church leaders sometimes struggle when asked to identify themselves. They may look back to what they are emerging *from* more than they look forward to what they are emerging *into*." Gibbs and Bolger, *Emerging Churches*, 28.

6. Rick McKinley, an emerging church pastor, has suggested that even asking the emerging church movement to define itself would be like asking a ten-year old to declare his college major.

7. Johnson, "Joyriding on the Downgrade," 212.

Protest: The Origins of the Emerging Church Movement

The Beginning of the Movement

During the 1980s and 1990s, generational theory influenced a number of young leaders to start church ministries that focused solely upon reaching a particular age group. Gen-X ministry, or ministry to the buster generation, became particularly popular during this time, and organizations such as the Leadership Network and Leighton Ford Ministries promoted well-attended conferences dedicated to Generation-X ministry. Especially influential was Dieter Zander, the planter of one of the first Gen-X churches in America.[8]

As the decade of the 1990s concluded, many of the young leaders involved in Gen-X ministry noticed substantial shifts starting to occur in Western culture. Gibbs and Bolger write that these young leaders came to believe "the evangelistic challenge for the church was not generational angst but a philosophical disconnect with wider culture."[9] While working for the Leadership Network, Doug Pagitt created an organization known as the Young Leader's Network in an attempt to address these new cultural shifts.[10] Pagitt's network included men such as Dan Kimball, Tony Jones, Mark Driscoll, Dieter Zander, and eventually Brian McLaren. Karen Ward, also a former leader in Gen-X ministry, reached conclusions similar to Pagitt's group and coined the term emerging church to describe these new leaders.[11]

---

8. Zander planted New Song in California and coauthored an influential book on Gen-X ministry. See Celek et al., *Inside the Soul of a New Generation*. Several emerging writers have cited Zander as an influential figure during their formative years.

9. Gibbs and Bolger, *Emerging Churches*, 32.

10. Tony Jones credits Pagitt's work in creating this network as the beginning of the emerging church movement. See his account in Jones, "Friendship, Faith, and Going Somewhere Together," 12.

11. Ward founded a website in 1999 entitled www.emerging-church.org, and many have traced the origins of the term emerging church to the founding of this website. Though Brian McLaren claims that he and Doug

Baptists and the Emerging Church Movement

Responding to a Changing Culture

These new emerging church leaders came to believe that the Western world has experienced a profound philosophical shift away from modernity in recent years. In short, modernity, a philosophical worldview with roots in Enlightenment thinking, places emphasis upon human reason and autonomy.[12] Emerging leader Dan Kimball has described it well by writing, "Pure modernism held to a single, universal worldview and moral standard, a belief that all knowledge is good and certain, truth is absolute, individualism is valued, and thinking, learning, and beliefs should be determined systematically and logically."[13]

According to emerging thought, as the West has shifted away from modernity it has embraced a new philosophical worldview known as postmodernity. Succinctly defining postmodernity presents a notoriously difficult task, partly because philosophers disagree over exactly what the term entails. Some philosophers speak of postmodernity as simply a continuation and expansion of modernity (i.e., hypermodernity), while others speak of postmodernity as a movement completely discontinuous with modernity.[14] Emerging writer Dan Kimball offers a brief description of postmodernity that represents how many emerging writers employ the term. Kimball claims that with postmodernity, "There

---

Pagitt created the term emerging church, it appears that Karen Ward's website predates McLaren's and Pagitt's work. McLaren offers his claim in McLaren, *Generous Orthodoxy*, 313.

12. Liederbach and Reid helpfully trace the Enlightenment roots of modernity and summarize modernity with the words: individualism, rationalism, and factualism. Liederbach and Reid, *Convergent Church*, 41.

13. Kimball, *Emerging Church*, 49.

14. Michael Horton, in his discussion with the emerging church, has described postmodernity simply as modernity taken to its logical conclusions, i.e., radical modernity or hypermodernity. See Horton, "Better Homes & Gardens," 105–25. By contrast, many emerging leaders appear to view postmodernity as a radical break from modernity. See, for example, Downing, *How Postmodernism Serves (My) Faith*. Downing's book has influenced many emerging leaders, and Brian McLaren has offered an endorsement that appears on the back cover.

is no single universal worldview. All truth is not absolute, community is valued over individualism, and thinking, learning, and beliefs can be determined nonlinearly."[15]

Protest against the Traditional Church

This shift from modernity to postmodernity forms the basis for the emerging church's protest against the traditional church. Emerging leaders allege that the traditional church has failed to understand and adequately respond to the West's new postmodern culture. They typically offer two arguments to support their complaint against the traditional church.

First, they accuse the traditional church of being ineffective because it holds to ministry methodologies that are rooted in modernity. In his book entitled *The Emerging Church*, Dan Kimball devotes eight chapters to just this point. Calling the shift to postmodernity "more than a generation gap," he writes that, despite the best efforts of traditional churches, "younger people for the most part are staying away from churches."[16] Kimball's book calls churches to embrace new forms of worship to reach young postmoderns.

Second, some emerging writers accuse the traditional church of allowing modernity to shape its theological and philosophical commitments. Brian McLaren in particular has repeatedly raised this issue. R. Scott Smith accurately summarizes McLaren's perspective when he writes that McLaren believes, "Just as modernity sought to conquer and control, whether that be through imperialistic efforts, technology, or the attempt to subjugate every aspect of life under science's dominion, so the [traditional] church has tended to adopt similar attitudes and even terminology."[17]

---

15. Kimball, *Emerging Church*, 57–58. The author has chosen Kimball's definition because it appears to capture what most in the emerging church movement believe at the popular level.

16. Kimball, *Emerging Church*, 48.

17. McLaren's sentences are sometimes long, wandering, and illusive. Smith's statement captures McLaren's views in a succinct manner. Smith, *Truth*

Ecclesiology: The Focus of the Emerging Church Movement

Liederbach and Reid therefore capture the intentions of emerging church leaders well when they define the emerging church movement as

> a groundswell of laypersons, ministers, theologians, and churches who are influenced by, and are responding to, real or perceived worldview shifts from modernity to postmodernity and who seek to make the Christian message relevant in the postmodern environment via shifts and adjustments in at least ministerial methodologies and usually theological/philosophical ideologies as well.[18]

In their definition, Liederbach and Reid note the two major areas in which emerging church leaders propose change: (1) ministry methodologies and (2) theological/philosophical ideologies. Because of the incredible diversity within the emerging movement, leaders within its ranks disagree whether changes to theological/philosophical commitments are actually necessary.[19] However, all emerging proponents agree that significant changes to ministry methodologies must occur. This shared conviction unites leaders such as Driscoll, Pagitt, Jones, and McLaren, as each insists that local church ministry must adapt to the culture's postmodern shift.

This emphasis on changing local church ministry leads emerging thinkers to make ecclesiology the primary concern of their movement. Many careful observers have noted the movement's ecclesiological focus. Scot McKnight has written, "At its core, the emerging movement is an attempt to fashion a new ecclesiology."[20]

---

and the New Kind of Christian, 54. McLaren's views on this subject are perhaps best detailed in three of his earlier volumes. See McLaren, *More Ready Than You Realize*; *New Kind of Christian*; and *Story We Find Ourselves In*.

18 Liederbach and Reid, *Convergent Church*, 19–20.

19. Leaders such as McLaren and Pagitt favor substantial changes to Christian theology, while more theologically conservative leaders such as Driscoll oppose such changes. See the following section on emerging church diversity for more information.

20. McKnight, "Five Streams of the Emerging Church," 37.

Understanding the Emerging Church Movement

Emerging church observers Ryan Bolger and Eddie Gibbs agree with McKnight's persepective. In 2005, they published the results of an extensive survey of American and British emerging churches.[21] While they cited a number of factors that categorized a church as emerging, Bolger summarized their conclusions by simply stating that the entire movement "is about ecclesiology."[22] Recently, some have gone so far as to state that the emerging church movement has such a strong emphasis on ecclesiology that it is akin to the desire for sweeping ecclesiological change exhibited by the early Baptists.[23]

Four Themes in Emerging Church Ecclesiology

This concentrated interest in ecclesiology means that the emerging church movement has offered a substantial amount of material in the area of ecclesiology. Research into emerging church ecclesiology can therefore prove a fruitful endeavor. Four aspects of church life in particular are of interest to emerging leaders: the church as community, the worship/preaching ministry of the church, the church's missional engagement, and leadership within the church.[24]

---

21. Gibbs and Bolger list nine practices common to emerging churches. It is interesting to note just how many impact a church's ecclesiology: (1) identification with the life of Jesus, (2) transformation of the secular realm, (3) living highly communal lives, (4) welcoming the stranger, (5) serving with generosity, (6) participating as producers, (7) creating as created beings, (8) leading as a body, (9) taking part in spiritual activities. See Gibbs and Bolger, *Emerging Churches*, 45.

22. The quote from Bolger in this paragraph is taken from an interview given to Jim Belcher. See Belcher, *Deep Church*, 44. Rejecting claims that the movement is primarily a philosophical or theological one, in the interview Bolger said, "I am not as concerned about denominations, particular views on postmodernism, or even theology [when attempting to define the movement] as much as I am about being a church that is missional, that cares for the poor and builds authentic community."

23. See Nelson, "Everything Old Is New Again."

24. After surveying emerging works, the author found emerging church works share an emphasis upon these four themes. These four central themes are similar to those discovered by John Hammett as detailed in Hammett, "Church according to Emergent/Emerging Church," 224-25.

11

Emerging church leaders emphasize these four areas because they believe each is important for reshaping church life in light of the culture's shift to postmodernity. While other aspects of emerging church ecclesiology certainly deserve examination, in this paper I will examine only these four themes because they appear most frequently in emerging works.

Diversity:
The Scope of the Emerging Church Movement

While emerging leaders were offering ambitious ecclesiological proposals, in the early 2000s most traditional church leaders had yet to hear of the emerging movement. It was D. A. Carson's 2005 publication entitled *Becoming Conversant with the Emerging Church* that helped to place the emerging movement at the center of popular evangelical discussion. When a respected evangelical academic discussed the movement in a best-selling book, it caught the attention of the evangelical world.

While Carson's book has sold well, it unfortunately did not accurately capture the wide diversity that exists within the emerging church movement. Carson's work offered excellent critiques of two of the movement's more radical leaders, yet it did not mention any of the movement's more theologically conservative spokespersons.[25] The bulk of Carson's work focused on troubling statements from leaders such as Brian McLaren and Steve Chalke, while it ignored the more profitable insights offered by leaders such as Mark Driscoll. Scot McKnight, in a rather substantial critique of Carson's work, stated, "Carson has foisted upon the evangelical world

---

25. Out of fairness, Carson makes it clear that his book will only focus on two significant leaders within the movement when he entitles a chapter, "Emerging Church Weaknesses Illustrated by Two Significant Books." However, his book's title, *Becoming Conversant with the Emerging Church*, gives the impression that the emerging church movement in total will receive consideration, and this leads to unnecessary confusion.

a stereotype [of the emerging movement] that most evangelicals are already prepared to reject."[26]

The critical response to Carson's book serves as a warning that all future conversations about the emerging church must be careful to take into account the movement's diversity. Soon after the publication of Carson's book, emerging church observers began to offer a number of taxonomies in an effort to adequately represent the movement's differences.[27] Of these taxonomies, none has become more influential than the one proposed by missiologist Ed Stetzer. Stetzer's work has received acceptance from a broad range of leaders within the emerging church movement, and it continues to offer helpful insights into the movement today.[28]

Stetzer's taxonomy divides the emerging movement into three major categories: relevants, reconstructionists, and revisionists.[29] Stetzer writes that relevants are "young (and not so young) leaders who some classify as 'emerging,' that are really just trying to make their worship, music, and outreach more contextual to emerging culture."[30] He notes, "Ironically, while some may consider them liberal, they are often deeply committed to biblical preaching, male pastoral leadership, and other values common in

---

26. Scot McKnight offers an extensive critique of Carson's work that is quite persuasive. McKnight, "What Is the Emerging Church?," 4–5.

27. For example, at the beginning of his proposed taxonomy Devine writes, "For those who know Carson's book, the justification for a new attempt at Evangelical engagement of the emerging church should be obvious—Carson's treatment passes over the doctrine-friendly stream of the movement." See Devine, "Emerging Church," 9. For a list of some of the proposed emerging church taxonomies, see Springer, "Hunting for Taxonomies."

28. Emerging church leader Andrew Jones expressed approval of Stetzer's formulation via a post on his personal blog. See Jones, "Ed Stetzer Gets It." Theologically conservative emerging church pastor Mark Driscoll also approved of Stetzer's work and incorporated it into his own thinking on the emerging church. See Driscoll, "Pastoral Perspective on the Emerging Church," 87–93.

29. Ed Stetzer, "First-Person: Understanding the Emerging Church," n.p.

30. Ibid.

conservative evangelical churches."[31] Mark Driscoll and Dan Kimball are members of this relevant stream of the movement.

Stetzer writes that the reconstructionists "think that the current form of church is frequently irrelevant and the structure [is] unhelpful."[32] Yet, he notes that reconstructionists do "typically hold to a more orthodox view of the Gospel and Scripture."[33] In an effort to correct the flaws they perceive in the traditional church, reconstructionists propose "more informal, incarnational, and organic church forms such as house churches."[34] The Australian writers Alan Hirsch and Michael Frost are members of this reconstructionist wing of the movement, as is the American writer Neil Cole.

Concerning the most radical wing of the movement, Stetzer writes that the revisionists "should be treated, appreciated, and read [in the same way] as we read mainline theologians."[35] He comes to this conclusion because many revisionists "are questioning (and in some cases denying) issues like the nature of the substitutionary atonement, the reality of hell, the complementarian nature of gender, and the nature of the Gospel itself."[36] Figures such as Brian McLaren, Karen Ward, and Doug Pagitt serve as prominent leaders in this revisionist stream.

Though Stetzer's categories have gained wide acceptance, some emerging church leaders and observers have attempted to add to Stetzer's work in an effort to bring even further clarity to the movement. Liederbach and Reid add a fourth category to Stetzer's taxonomy entitled roamers. They define roamers as people who "roam about, more displeased with how things are than sure of what to believe or where to settle."[37] In addition, Mark Driscoll suggests a new category entitled Reformed relevants. With this

---

31. Ibid.
32. Ibid.
33. Ibid.
34. Driscoll, "Pastoral Perspective on the Emergent Church," 90.
35. Stetzer, "First-Person," n.p.
36. Ibid.
37. Liederbach and Reid, *Convergent Church*, 102.

category, he hopes to highlight those within the movement who hold to a reformed understanding of soteriology.[38]

While these new categories aptly describe some in the movement, neither offers anything particularly useful for discussions pertaining to emerging ecclesiology. The roamers mentioned by Liederbach and Reid do not consistently participate in church life, so they offer few serious ecclesiological proposals. Driscoll's emphasis upon soteriology is interesting, but few serious ecclesiological differences exist between reformed relevants and non-reformed relevants. Therefore, for this work, I will make use the three categories offered by Stetzer.

Relevance: The Importance of the Emerging Church Movement

The popularity of the emerging church movement reached its peak in the mid-2000s and has experienced a rapid decline since that time. This fact has led some observers to conclude that the movement has died. Writing for *World Magazine*, Anthony Bradley states, "Reading a new book or going to a conference about the emerging church is a waste of time and money unless it's to understand the movement as a recent historical one. The emerging church movement has ended."[39] Bradley believes the emerging movement's lifespan occurred between the short years of 1989–2010. Popular emerging church blogger Andrew Jones agrees with Bradley's conclusion. In a blog entry, Jones wrote, "In my opinion, 2009 marks the year when the emerging church suddenly and decisively ceased to be a radical and controversial movement in global Christianity."[40] With such a clear decline in interest, some may begin to question

---

38. Phil Johnson notes that at the 2006 Desiring God Conference, Mark Driscoll cited Stetzer's three categories and then created a fourth category entitled reformed relevants. Driscoll placed himself in this fourth category. See Johnson, "Joyriding on the Downgrade," 212n3.

39. Bradley, "Farewell Emerging Church, 1989–2010."

40. Jones, "Emerging Church Movement (1989–2009)?"

whether a research project on the emerging church has any merit.[41] However, I believe that new research into the emerging movement will still prove to be profitable, and three factors have persuaded me of the emerging movement's continued relevance.

An Influential Movement

First, during its prime, the emerging church movement enjoyed tremendous influence. Scot McKnight has written:

> If you are serious enough to contemplate major trends in the Church today, at an international level, and if you define emerging as many of us do—in missional, or ecclesiology terms, rather than epistemological ones—then you will learn quickly enough that there is a giant elephant in the middle of the Church's living room. It is the emerging church movement and it is a definite threat to traditional evangelical ecclesiology.[42]

While McKnight unfortunately decided to use the word *threat* to describe the emerging church's relationship to the traditional church, he does correctly state that the movement was much larger and influential than many evangelicals first realized. At the start of the twenty-first century, many Christian churches and leaders were actively involved in reconsidering their ecclesiological structures in light of the perceived rise of postmodernity.[43]

---

41. This author agrees with Bradley and Jones that the emerging movement's popularity has significantly declined. However, some conversations related to the movement continue, so it is perhaps a little premature to declare the movement completely dead. For example, the respected British newsmagazine the *Economist* somewhat recently reported on a well-attended emerging church festival that occurred in North Carolina. See Economist Staff, "Christian Festivals: A Broader Church," 26. In addition, Brazos Press recently published a book that details the emerging church movement. See Corcoran, *Church in the Present Tense*. Finally, Ross Douthat, a conservative columnist for the *New York Times*, recently highlighted the emerging church movement in his best-selling *Bad Religion*. Douthat, *Bad Religion*, 279–80, 286.

42. McKnight, "What Is the Emerging Church?," 9.

43. In this paper, I will limit my discussion only to leaders and churches

Understanding the Emerging Church Movement

The emerging church movement's popularity during this time allowed it to influence the ecclesiology of many younger evangelicals. Many evangelical seminarians and youth pastors were exposed to emerging thought during the movement's peak. Some of those influenced, including young Baptists, appear to have accepted emerging church proposals uncritically. This fact means that though the term emerging may have lost popularity, many younger evangelicals seem to still cling to aspects of emerging ecclesiology.[44] A careful examination of emerging ecclesiology will therefore have value, as these younger evangelicals did not receive one during the movement's prime.

A Continuing Movement

Second, much of the emerging church discussion continues, simply under a different moniker. Recently, a number of authors and bloggers have dedicated their ministry discussions to the creation of missional churches. This missional church discussion has become so large that one evangelical observer has stated, "Over the last few years, there has been no bigger buzzword in Christianity than missional."[45] Some missional church proponents advocate ecclesiological proposals similar to those proposed by the emerging church, and the similarities between these two movements have

---

that have publicly identified themselves with the emerging church movement. However, it is important to recognize that many thinkers with no *official* connection to the emerging community were involved in discussions similar to those that occurred within the movement. Carson, for example, writes that it has become easy to find church leaders "who do not think of themselves as belonging to the emerging church movement who nevertheless share most of its values and priorities." Carson, *Becoming Conversant*, 9.

44. Andrew Jones is one of many who have made this observation. He argues that though the emerging movement has died, it in some ways continues to live because its previous followers now exert influence upon traditional church denominations. See Jones, "Emerging Church Movement."

45. McCracken, "Church in a 'Missional' Age." See also McCracken's recent assessment of the latest "cool" trends in contemporary Christianity in which he writes, "Missional has overtaken emerging as the defining buzzword of cool Christianity." See McCracken, *Hipster Christianity*, 151.

prompted some emerging leaders to simply rebrand themselves as missional.[46] A study of emerging church ecclesiology will therefore offer insight into certain aspects of the current missional church discussion.

A Movement of Concern to Baptists

Finally, Baptists of all people should concern themselves with new ecclesiological proposals. From their beginning, Baptists have drawn their unique identity from their ecclesiological distinctives. Because emerging church leaders propose substantial changes to church life and structure, Baptists should seek to understand and assess these new proposals. Baptists should provide a charitable response when emerging ecclesiology contradicts Baptist thought. However, Baptists can also possess a humble readiness to accept emerging proposals that agree with their ecclesiology so that they might potentially profit from them.

Conclusion

The emerging movement is a group of diverse leaders attempting to minister in our current cultural context. Though discussions concerning epistemology appear in emerging literature, emerging leaders are primarily concerned with ecclesiology. They may hold to different beliefs concerning theology and methodology, but a shared desire to reshape church life in light of the rise of postmodernity unites them. Evangelicals, and Baptists in particular, should carefully examine their proposals. In the following chapters, I will examine the ecclesiological proposals of emerging writers and focus on the four areas of interest to them: community, preaching/worship, missional engagement, and leadership.

---

46. Mark Driscoll serves as an example of this trend. He argues that the terms emerging and missional are now practically synonymous. See Driscoll, *Religion Saves*, 210. See also Driscoll, *Radical Reformission*, 17–18.

2

Assessing Emerging Church Community

The Emerging Desire for Community

EMERGING CHURCH LEADERS ARE particularly concerned with creating authentic and accepting communities. After conducting an extensive, multiyear study of emerging churches in the United States and the UK, Fuller Seminary professors Eddie Gibbs and Ryan Bolger concluded that emerging church leaders have a strong desire to live "highly communal lives."[1] This deep-seated aspiration for community has two sources. First, emerging leaders, to varying degrees, have embraced postmodern thought and its attendant emphasis upon community.[2] Second, emerging leaders bemoan the loss of community that many people in the modern world tend to experience.[3] Dan Kimball articulates the emerging

1. Gibbs and Bolger, *Emerging Churches*, 45.

2. Concerning the postmodern emphasis upon community, and its implications for ministry, Stanley J. Grenz offers a helpful statement. He writes, "We can no longer follow the lead of modernity and position the individual at center stage. Instead, we must remind ourselves that our faith is highly social ... Our Gospel must address the human person within the context of the communities in which people are imbedded." Grenz, *Primer on Postmodernism*, 168–69.

3. For an excellent examination on the loss of sense of community in contemporary America, consider Putnam, *Bowling Alone*. This work has received

mindset well when he writes, "Because emerging generations live in this confusing and often disappointing world, we need a much more relational approach to ministry and evangelism."[4]

Emerging church proponents believe that the traditional church model simply does not offer the authentic and accepting atmosphere that young postmoderns desire.[5] Mark Devine notes that this issue of community is actually one of the key protests that the emerging church movement has with the traditional church.[6] The writings of Spencer Burke offer an example of the type of strong language sometimes used in this protest. Calling traditional church fellowship "spiritual McCarthyism" and life in the evangelical subculture "spiritual isolationism," Burke believes that the traditional church model "encourages people to orchestrate their lives to avoid censure and minimize risk. In short, it teaches people to live life in fear—to put up or shut up."[7]

As they desire to withdraw from the perceived failures of the traditional church model, emerging leaders propose new models of church that "attempt to provide safe places for unbelievers and spiritual seekers to consider the claims of Christ in an atmosphere characterized by patience and openness."[8] In this chapter, after a brief survey of Baptist convictions related to the church, I will present popular emerging church proposals related church

---

praise from leaders such as Mark Driscoll.

4. Kimball, *Emerging Church*, 81.

5. For example, Dan Kimball details how today's young, postmodern generation perceives the traditional church. He notes that most of their opinions concerning the church are not positive, and many view the church as arrogant, judgmental, and even oppressive. In light of this, he suggests a new, emerging church model that he believes will provide an attractive community for young postmoderns. See Kimball, *They Like Jesus but Not the Church*. See also the personal testimonies of emerging leaders compiled by Gibbs and Bolger. Many of these convey a sense of disillusionment with the feeling of community available within traditional churches. Gibbs and Bolger, *Emerging Churches*, 239–328.

6. Devine, "Emerging Church," 9–11.

7. Burke, "From the Third Floor," 31.

8. Devine, "Emerging Church," 11.

community. I will then assess these proposals from historic Baptist convictions about the nature of the church.

Baptist Convictions about Church Life

Many of the emerging church proposals intended to create authentic community directly affect a church's ecclesiological convictions. Because of this, it will be necessary to briefly survey historic Baptist ecclesiology so that the reader may have a standard by which to evaluate emerging thought. Baptists should pay close attention to new ecclesiological proposals, however well intentioned they are, because Baptists have historically defined themselves by their ecclesiological convictions. Chief among these convictions is the doctrine of regenerate church membership. John Hammett has written, "Central to the Baptist vision of the church is the insistence that the church must be composed of believers only."[9] As Baptists have held this conviction since their very inception, one cannot legitimately label a church as Baptist if it does not seek to encourage a regenerate membership.[10]

The Somerset Confession of 1656 speaks of the need for Baptist churches to carefully work to promote a regenerate church body:

> In admitting of members into the church of Christ, it is the duty of the church, and ministers whom it concerns, in faithfulness to God, that they be careful they receive none but such as do make forth evident demonstration of the new birth, and the work of faith with power.[11]

Baptists have historically employed a number of practices to enable the kind of protection encouraged by the Somerset Confession.

---

9. Hammett, *Biblical Foundations*, 81.

10. Leon McBeth directly ties regenerate church membership to Baptist origins when he writes, "Perhaps the origin of Baptists is best explained as a search for a pure church. They sought a church composed of 'visible saints,' that is, true believers." McBeth, *Baptist Heritage*, 75.

11. Somerset Confession as recorded in Lumpkin, *Baptist Confessions of Faith*, 211.

Baptists and the Emerging Church Movement

Three such practices are worthy of consideration here, because they directly relate to recent emerging church proposals. First, Baptists have required prospective members to make a public profession of faith before receiving admittance into the church. Baptists consider the act of believer's baptism a crucial component of this public profession. Historic Baptist confessions express this belief, and the Baptist Faith and Message 2000 follows this trajectory by defining baptism as

> an act of obedience *symbolizing* the believer's faith in a crucified, buried, and risen Savior, the believer's death to sin, the burial of the old life, and the resurrection to walk in newness of life in Christ Jesus. It is a *testimony to his faith* in the final resurrection of the dead. Being a church ordinance it is *prerequisite to the privileges of church membership and to the Lord's Supper.*[12]

Second, most Baptists have sought to maintain a clearly defined church membership in order to distinguish between the member (who should be regenerate) and the non-member (who may not be regenerate). Mark Dever writes, "In Baptist history, pastors have recognized the vigorous practice of membership, not only as a matter of prudence but also of principle."[13] Mike McKinley, a young Baptist church planter, succinctly explains the value he sees in a clearly defined membership by writing, "If Christians are supposed to be different from the world, and if the church is meant to be a group of Christians committed to each other for the glory of God, it's essential that we know who 'we' are."[14]

Third, Baptists have typically formed church covenants and statements of faith in order to express the expectation that church

---

12. Southern Baptist Convention, "Baptist Faith and Message 2000," n.p., emphasis added. Obviously, the Baptist Faith and Message 2000 does not represent the convictions of all Baptists. However, the document does serve as an influential confessional statement for one of the largest Baptist bodies in the world, the Southern Baptist Convention.

13. Dever, "Regaining Meaningful Church Membership," 53. For a brief historical survey of Baptist views on church membership, see Finn, "Historical Analysis," 66–67.

14. McKinley, *Church Planting Is for Wimps*, 58.

members live their lives as regenerate people.[15] John Hammett notes that Baptists believe "one of the major purposes for the use of church covenants is precisely to safeguard regenerate church membership."[16] If a member consistently fails to abide by the church's recognized expectations, Baptists have argued that such a member must be removed from the church in order to preserve the regenerate nature of the church body.

These three practices are present in Baptist theology today though they are not always present in local church practice. The Baptist Faith and Message 2000 implies all three practices in its definition of the church by stating the church is, "An autonomous local congregation of *baptized believers, associated by covenant* in the faith and fellowship of the Gospel."[17] The phrase "baptized believers" makes obvious reference to a public profession of faith via believer's baptism. The phrase "associated by covenant" refers to a clearly defined church membership united by a shared commitment to a church covenant.

Several emerging church leaders associated with the movement's relevant stream attempt to provide seekers with an inviting atmosphere that still maintains Baptist ecclesiology.[18] However, the desire to create an accepting community has led some reconstructionist and revisionist leaders to propose church structures that are unhealthy from a Baptist perspective. Such leaders "reject formal demarcation between believers and nonbelievers, eschew formal church membership altogether, and assume a

---

15. For a historical survey of the role of covenants have played in Baptist church life, see Deweese, *Baptist Church Covenants*. In addition, consider Renihan, *Edification and Beauty*, 48–52.

16. Hammett, "Regenerate Church Membership," 34.

17. Southern Baptist Convention, "Baptist Faith and Message 2000," emphasis added.

18. Relevants Mark Driscoll or Dan Kimball serve as examples of those who offer proposals that are friendly to a Baptistic understanding of the church. Devine describes the relevants of the emerging church movement by writing, "Many doctrine-friendly emerging churches attempt to provide a safe place for unbelievers while maintaining covenant-shaped, church discipline-regulated membership within their congregations." See Devine, "Emerging Church," 11.

belonging-before-believing posture toward all comers."[19] It is therefore fitting to assess how such proposals might affect the three Baptist practices intended to preserve a regenerate body: the public profession of faith via believer's baptism, clearly defined church membership, and shared life in a covenantal community.

Public Professions

A book on evangelism popular among some emerging church leaders states, "Most people today will come to faith in the context of a community. Belonging comes before believing. Evangelism today is about helping people belong so that they can come to believe."[20] This statement briefly describes an ecclesiological position known as the belonging-before-belief model. Emerging church observer Jim Belcher offers a succinct definition of this model when he writes, "Simply put, the emerging church does not like the traditional church's insistence that belief (adherence to certain doctrines) must precede belonging (being part of the community)."[21]

Many revisionist leaders express a preference for the belonging-before-belief model, and Gibbs and Bolger document this fact in their chapter entitled "Welcoming the Stranger."[22] To their credit, advocates of this model correctly analyze a trend pres-

---

19. Ibid.

20. Richardson, *Reimagining Evangelism*, 50. Several emerging leaders have expressed appreciation for this book, and Brian McLaren authored its foreword.

21. Belcher, *Deep Church*, 94.

22. See Gibbs and Bolger, *Emerging Churches*, 117–34. In addition, though not all emerging church leaders use the phrasing of "belonging-before-belief," one can certainly find the concept present in much of their thinking. For example, the theme is clearly present in several of Brian McLaren's works. See in particular McLaren, *New Kind of Christian*. One must also note that the belonging-before-belief model is not entirely unique to the emerging church movement. It does appear, albeit in a more modest form, in a number of non-emerging works. See, for example, Murray, *Church after Christendom*, 10–23; and Hunter, *Celtic Way of Evangelism*.

Assessing Emerging Church Community

ently occurring in much of Western culture. Most postmoderns will likely desire to belong to a group before they fully affirm its teachings.[23] Unfortunately, many of these leaders go too far in their desire to accommodate this culture shift. For example, emerging pastor Tim Conder bluntly states, "We need to strongly question the importance of placing any barriers at the church's doors."[24]

Especially troubling is Conder's attack upon the traditional practice of using doctrinal beliefs as a determining factor in admitting someone into church membership. Conder writes, "I believe that allowing doctrine to dominate the process of joining Christian community is theologically, functionally, and missionally challenged."[25] Instead of a shared theological commitment, Conder argues that the church should simply formulate itself around a shared commitment to life together as a missional community. He says that if a list of evaluative questions is to exist for newcomers, it should begin with the question, "Does this person share in and contribute to our mission in an appropriate and authentic manner?"[26] Though Conder is willing to consider a person's

---

23. For a brief explanation as to why this is a current cultural trend, see Richardson, *Reimagining Evangelism*, 50–54. Many thinkers not associated with the emerging church have also recognized this trend. See Stetzer and Putman, *Breaking the Missional Code*, 104–7.

24. Conder, *Church in Transition*, 150. The phrase "church doors" here refers to membership and joining the church community, not just attending a church worship service. Conder's views are worthy of attention because: (1) he is an emerging writer who has written extensively on this subject, and (2) his work in this area represents the beliefs of many within the emerging church. For example, commenting specifically upon Conder's belonging-before-belief model, Jim Belcher stated, "I think Tim's views on conversion represent most camps in the emerging church." Belcher, *Deep Church*, 94.

25. Conder, *Church in Transition*, 146. Revisionist Tony Jones agrees with Conder on this point. Jones has written, "Statements of faith [in churches] are about drawing borders, which means you have to load your weapons and place soldiers at those borders. You have to check people's passports when they enter those borders. It becomes an obsession—guarding the borders. That is simply not the ministry of Jesus. It wasn't the ministry of Paul or Peter." From an interview with *Relevant Magazine*, July/August 2006, cited in DeYoung and Kluck, *Why We're Not Emergent*, 117.

26. Conder, "Existing Church/Emerging Church Matrix," 102.

ethics and lifestyle as part of this missional evaluation, his model remains deficient. In particular, he chides traditional churches for their reluctance to admit anyone into membership who cannot "profess an evangelical description of their faith."[27]

Spencer Burke, a revisionist leader formerly in the Baptist tradition, shares Conder's sentiments. Burke founded a popular emerging blog entitled *TheOoze.com* in the late 1990s. He writes that he started his blog with the goal of creating a place where

> the various parts of the faith community are like mercury. At times we'll roll together; at times we'll roll apart. Try to touch the liquid or constrain it, and the substance will resist. Rather than force people to fall into line, an oozy community tolerates differences and treats people who hold opposing views with great dignity.[28]

Burke states that this model of communal living is "the essence of the emerging church."[29] D. A. Carson explains that for Burke, the church should exist as a formless community in which people "voice their opinions and interact with each other without anyone being 'up' or 'down,' or 'right' or wrong.'"[30] Taking his beliefs to their logical conclusion, Burke questions why Baptists have historically withheld church privileges such as communion from unbelievers. He suggests that allowing an unbeliever to partake of communion might allow the unbeliever "a powerful first experience with the glory of Christ."[31]

Historically, Baptists have argued that a person should not become a full member of a church, or share in communion, until

---

27. Conder, *Church in Transition*, 146.
28. Burke, "From the Third Floor," 36–37.
29. Ibid.
30. Carson, *Becoming Conversant*, 146. One must note that Burke has recently removed himself from participation in a local church. He has written, "To be honest, religion doesn't really work for me anymore. Being aligned with an institutional church or a particular system of worship seems increasingly irrelevant to my ongoing journey with God." Burke and Taylor, *Heretic's Guide to Eternity*, 6.
31. Burke, "From the Third Floor," 30–31.

Assessing Emerging Church Community

after his or her conversion. They contend a person should testify to his or her conversion by publicly affirming the gospel through the act of believer's baptism, an act that is, to use Conder's words, an "evangelical description of their faith."[32] Yet, some of the more radical proponents of the belonging-before-belief model clearly advocate allowing an unbeliever full entrance into the life of the church. This should be of deep concern to Baptist thinkers who wish to uphold the Baptist distinctive of regenerate church membership. Convictional Baptists should not follow emerging leaders on this point.

However, though a radical implementation of the belonging-before-belief model would be flawed from a Baptist perspective, emerging leaders are right in their desire to create an accepting church community. Baptist churches can learn from the emerging church movement about the need to create a hospitable atmosphere for unbelievers while taking caution to retain their ecclesiological convictions.

Baptist authors Ed Stetzer and David Putman offer a proposal that would do just that.[33] They recommend that churches be "proactive about creating specific experiences for those who are on the journey [i.e., spiritual seekers]."[34] Their model allows non-members to participate in church life by performing non-spiritual acts of service and participating in many of the social events of the church. However, their model also emphasizes the need for conversion and for a public profession of faith. In their approach, "each step toward the cross is celebrated as a victory."[35] When an unbeliever does become converted, Stetzer and Putman encourage

---

32. Conder, *Church in Transition*, 146.

33. Stetzer and Putman, *Breaking the Missional Code*, 104–7. Mark Driscoll, a member of the relevant stream of the emerging church movement, follows a similar pattern of ministry. His most complete work on ecclesiology is Driscoll and Breshears, *Vintage Church*.

34. Stetzer and Putman, *Breaking the Missional Code*, 105.

35. Ibid.

churches to be "serious about conversion and make a big deal about people going public with their faith."[36]

Clearly Defined Church Membership

Other emerging church proposals touch on the Baptist requirement that churches possess a clearly defined membership. Emerging leaders who have written on this subject believe that church membership categories of in and out hinder acceptance and authenticity. For example, Rob Bell has written, "It is when the church gives itself away in radical acts of service and compassion expecting nothing in return that the way of Jesus is most vividly put on display. To do this, the church must stop thinking of everybody primarily in categories of in or out, saved or not, believer or nonbeliever."[37] Several emerging models of church life explicitly attempt to do away with church membership. Three such proposals are worthy of consideration here because of their popularity: the centered-set approach, the organic church model, and Peter Ward's liquid church model.

The Centered-Set Model

Reconstructionist leaders Michael Frost and Alan Hirsch are the leading advocates for the centered-set model.[38] In their influen-

---

36. Ibid.

37. Rob Bell, *Velvet Elvis*, 167.

38. Frost and Hirsch, *Shaping of Things to Come*. This centered-set model is by no means unique to Frost and Hirsch, and it actually predates their work in *The Shaping of Things to Come*. However, I have chosen to deal solely with Frost and Hirsch's formulation of the model because Frost and Hirsch are popular emerging writers who have addressed this issue relatively recently. For a demonstration of the popularity of the Frost and Hirsch's work, consider a blog post in which emerging leader Andrew Jones declared *The Shaping of Things to Come* to be the second-most important book one can read on the emerging church movement. See Jones, "Fifty Books on My Emerging Church Bookshelf." For work on the centered-set model that predates Frost and Hirsch, see Hiebert, *Anthropological Reflections on Missiological Issues*,

Assessing Emerging Church Community

tial work *The Shaping of Things to Come*, they describe the traditional church as existing in a bounded-set model. They define the bounded-set model as "a set of people clearly marked off from those who do not belong to it."[39] They specifically mention church membership as an example of this boundary mentality.

Churches in the future, they argue, must move from a bounded-set model to a centered-set model in order to show hospitality to spiritual seekers. They write, "This means that rather than drawing a border to determine who belongs and who doesn't, a centered-set is defined by its core values, and people are not seen as in or out, but as closer or further away from the center."[40] Frost and Hirsch describe Christ as the center of this model, and argue that "rather than seeing people as Christian or non-Christian, as in or out, we should see people by their degree of distance from the center, Christ."[41]

Frost and Hirsch believe that their model benefits seekers because it "acknowledges the contribution of not-yet-Christians to Christian community and values the contribution by all people."[42] Emerging writer Ray Anderson agrees with their conclusion. He

---

107–36; and Guder, *Missional Church*, 183–220. The centered-set model also appears in popular books not commonly associated with the emerging church movement, such as Petersen, *Church without Walls*, 173–75.

39. Frost and Hirsch, *Shaping of Things to Come*, 47.

40. Ibid. Frost and Hirsch define centered-set and bounded-set in a manner consistent with other leaders in the reconstructionist and revisionist streams of the emerging church movement. For example, revisionist leader Phyllis Tickle describes the bounded-set mentality by writing, "It requires adherence to certain rules of doctrinal belief and human conduct as prerequisites to membership." She contrasts this stance with the centered-set approach, which she describes by writing, "In center-set Christianity, one simply belongs to a gathering of Christians by virtue of a shared humanity and an affinity with the individuals involved in whatever the group as a whole is doing." Commenting on the popularity of the centered-set approach in the emerging church movement, Tickle writes, "By the change of the millennium [twenty-first century], emergent Christianity in general had adopted a center-set approach." See Tickle, *Great Emergence*, 158–59.

41. Frost and Hirsch, *Shaping of Things to Come*, 47.

42. Ibid.

too advocates the centered-set model out of a belief that it will lead to a more accepting church community. He writes:

> And if grace is to be the mark of emerging churches, it must be an amazing grace, grace that embraces moral and spiritual ambiguity for the sake of bringing persons to a greater dimension of human wholeness. This will not be easy. The boundary of emerging churches will of necessity need to be porous and somewhat ambiguous even as the center is truthful.[43]

These writers have a commendable desire that the church be welcoming to nonbelievers. However, their employment of the centered-set proposal intentionally removes any categories of in and out, including the category of church membership. Therefore, this use of the centered-set model becomes problematic for convictional Baptists who seek to preserve a regenerate church body through the practice of church membership. Indeed, when Frost and Hirsch state, "We should see people by their degree of separation from the center [Christ],"[44] the reader should not view this statement as implying anything akin to church membership. In this employment of the centered-set model, no clear and official differentiation can exist between the different types of people who participate in the communal life of the church.

The Structureless Model

Out of a desire for a more authentic community, some revisionist leaders have proposed a church model completely devoid of any structure or organization.[45] Mark Scandrette describes the structureless nature of his ministry ReIMAGINE! when he states, "It didn't make sense to be intentional about spiritual things anymore. For some reason, we just needed to be real and be friends and to

---

43. Anderson, *Emergent Theology for Emerging Churches*, 156.
44. Frost and Hirsch, *Shaping of Things to Come*, 47.
45. No universally recognized name exists for this model. In this work, I have adopted the name structureless model to portray the model's resistance to any type of ecclesiological structure.

let something develop naturally."[46] His community has no official name, no official meeting place, and "no one is officially in or out."[47] Spencer Burke, also an advocate of this model, believes that very loose affiliation will allow churches to develop a more natural rhythm than the traditional model.[48]

Emerging churches operating within this mindset will typically choose no officially recognized day, time, or place to meet. Instead, natural connections are expected to simply arise spontaneously between church participants throughout the week.[49] These loose, informal connections usually involve only a few people and occur at a popular social location for young adults. Mark Driscoll describes his experience with this phenomenon by writing:

> In my multiple personal conversations over the past decade with some well-known leaders of the more left-leaning fringe of the emerging church, they have explained that they find their definition of the church more in what we do rather than in what Jesus has done. They talk about how two guys drinking beer are "church" if in their hearts their time at the pub is spiritual. One well-known international missiologist told me that his friends stopped going to church and instead water-ski together

---

46. This statement is taken form an interview with Scandrette recorded in Gibbs and Bolger, *Emerging Churches*, 103–4.

47. Ibid.

48. Ibid. While Burke and Scandrette are two prominent advocates of this model, there are other emerging leaders who also make statements that appear to advocate for a form of church life devoid of structure. For example, consider Joseph R. Myers who advocates for a model entitled "responsible anarchy" in Myers, *Organic Community*, 23–67. Also, consider the "bottom-up" and "decentralized" model found in Brewin, *Signs of Emergence*, 73–118.

49. The idea of a church completely devoid of any structure is no doubt difficult for those within the traditional church to understand. Gibbs and Bolger helpfully describe the differences between the traditional model and this more organic approach by writing, "The Sunday worship service was the most obvious entry point into the traditional church and perhaps the most straightforward way of ascribing its identity. But the emerging church is a different animal. Many of the groups that started recently are meetingless in this sense. They have moved away from a central gathering. They are relational, organic, and flowing." Gibbs and Bolger, *Emerging Churches*, 102.

every Sunday, and he told them that was fine because being together in the boat was a kingdom activity and therefore qualified as church.[50]

This organic model of church life presents serious and obvious problems to a Baptistic understanding of the church. No defined membership roster exists in these communities, and the rejection of any semblance of structure makes it difficult to determine exactly who the church "is." Without having any mechanism to recognize who is in and who is out of the community, the church has no way to preserve a regenerate body.

In fact, it is legitimate to question whether the communities that arise in this model are actually churches at all. A church certainly consists of more than several close friends gathering at various times throughout the week to discuss spiritual concerns. Kevin DeYoung offers a helpful insight on this point when he writes:

> I have no problem with defining the church as elect people of God, or as the gathered Christian community, or as all those who have put their faith in Jesus. These are pretty standard definitions. But to say the church is the people of God is not the same as saying that wherever the people of God are there you have a church . . . the church [universal] manifests itself in churches. And, churches do certain things and are marked by certain characteristics.[51]

The structureless model championed by emerging writers indeed lacks many of the necessary characteristics of a church. Chief among them, it lacks the intention to actually be a publicly identifiable church. Emerging proponents of this model content themselves with meeting one another randomly, and they express strong sentiment against the notion that they should become a unified body that publicly takes on the mantle of church. Stetzer

---

50. Driscoll and Breshears, *Vintage Church*, 53. The fact that Driscoll offers this criticism indicates that this proposal is not universal among emerging church proponents and is only popular with the "left-leaning fringe," i.e., the revisionists.

51. DeYoung and Kluck, *Why We Love the Church*, 166.

and Towns correctly warn such thinkers that "meeting together does not make one a church—meeting together with the intent of being a church does."[52]

The Liquid Church Model

Peter Ward, a professor at King's College in London, offers his liquid church model also out of a desire for greater authenticity and connectedness. While Ward does not officially identify himself as part of the emerging church movement, the tone of his proposals certainly resonate with the movement, and his model has influenced many revisionist emerging church leaders.[53] Leaders such as Karen Ward, Spencer Burke, and Kester Brewin have all stated that Ward's liquid church model has shaped their ministry methodologies.[54]

Similar to structureless church proponents, Ward suggests that the church does not need to have an officially recognized

---

52. Towns and Stetzer, *Perimeters of Light*, 70. Obviously, it takes more than meeting with the intention of being a church for a group to become a true church. Yet, Towns and Stetzer are correct to note that a true church will not be less than this. Jonathan Leeman has helpfully noted that a true church will embrace Christ's mission for the church and the authority structures Christ gives to the church in Matthew chapters 16, 18, and 28. Naming these texts the church's charter, Leeman writes, "We must maintain the distinction between a local church and a group of Christians. The difference lies precisely in the fact that Christ has handed a charter of authority [i.e., the commands in Matt. 16, 18, 28] to the church, not to Christians generically." Leeman, *Church and the Surprising Offense of God's Love*, 204.

53. For example, Carson writes, "It is not surprising that many books and articles that do not identify themselves as part of the emerging church movement nevertheless share its core values and thus belong to it without the label. One thinks, for instance, of Peter Ward's *Liquid Church*." Carson, *Becoming Conversant*, 13.

54. These emerging leaders claim that Ward's book has influenced their thinking in an interview with Gibbs and Bolger. See Gibbs and Bolger, *Emerging Churches*, 113–15. In addition, commenting on the liquid church model, Belcher writes, "I believe his [Ward's] thinking captures the thoughts of a large segment of the emerging church and continues to drive the conversation in many parts of the emerging world." Belcher, *Deep Church*, 164.

public meeting. He writes, "I suggest that we need to shift from seeing church as a gathering of people meeting in one place at one time—that is, a congregation—to a notion of church as a series of relationships and communications."[55] Ward argues for this position because he believes, like structureless church proponents, that the traditional model of weekly meetings is not conducive or attractive to a postmodern generation desiring authenticity.

However, substantial differences do exist between Ward's model and the structureless church model. The structureless model desires to replace regular church meetings with informal and seemingly random connections. Ward's liquid church model desires to replace traditional church meetings with a loosely affiliated network of nodes, fellowship groups based around shared interests and concerns. Participants involved in the liquid church model continually create new nodes as their needs and interests change, and it is this fluidity that has prompted Ward to entitle his model *liquid* church.

Ward believes that informal connections should develop between several of these different nodes so that a network can form. He defines the church as a network of these loosely connected nodes. According to Ward, the various nodes involved in a shared network should occasionally meet at a specified "hub" for mutual fellowship and encouragement. This hub should not be a church building, but should instead be a place that all the members consider interesting. Ward writes, "A hub might be a retreat center, a sports team, a music group, a record company, a Christian shop, and so on."[56] This networked connection between the nodes is not to be firm, and the various nodes do appear to be autonomous.

Ward argues that this loose confederation of nodes, each centered upon a different interest and cause, represents the proper model for church in our postmodern culture. To offer an example of how this proposal might look, Ward asks his readers to consider the "various productive and creative processes that characterize contemporary Christian culture. By this I mean festivals, worship

55. Ward, *Liquid Church*, 2.
56. Ibid., 87.

music, evangelism courses, and other processes."[57] Ward then states, "As these individuals, organizations, and groups carry out their activities they are being or doing church."[58] In Ward's model then, church exists when people form different groups (i.e., nodes) around a common interest and then loosely align their groups together in order to support a common cause or to have fellowship with one another.

While Ward labels his proposal a theory, several revisionist leaders in both the United States and the UK have attempted to implement parts or all of his proposal.[59] Per Ward's suggestions, participants in these churches meet in different nodes at various times throughout the week. These nodes provide fellowship around a common interest and an opportunity to perform social work.[60] The individual nodes then occasionally join at some point in time to form a larger meeting with other nodes in the network (i.e., the church). Karen Ward has deep praise for this approach because she believes it combines both intimate community and structure. Furthermore, she argues that the structures that do develop are created naturally "as they are required by the Gospel."[61]

Ward's proposal is creative and sincere. However, for two reasons it presents potential problems for any church that desires to maintain a regenerate membership. First, as with several other emerging proposals, the liquid church model intentionally seeks to remove any notion of church membership from the life of the church. Ward writes:

57. Ibid.

58. Ibid.

59. Gibbs and Bolger offer a section in which emerging leaders describe how they have attempted to implement Ward's liquid church model into their ministries. See Gibbs and Bolger, *Emerging Churches*, 113–15.

60. Emerging writer Spencer Burke has labeled these nodes "slices." In Burke's view, "all the church doesn't necessarily need to get together for each meeting." Rather, several slices (i.e., nodes) meet regularly for a more intimate time of community. See his interview in Gibbs and Bolger, *Emerging Churches*, 113–14.

61. Karen Ward states this in an interview recorded in Gibbs and Bolger, *Emerging Churches*, 113.

> When we start to regard the network itself as a church, then the notion of insiders and outsiders starts to break down. Instead, we have a network of communication and relationship where Christian love and mutual support form part of the flow. The boundaries have started to become fuzzy and less well defined.[62]

Ward later argues that this process of creating a "fuzzy and less well defined" membership is a good thing:

> Liquid church will see this kind of fuzzy aspect of networks as an advantage. It means that around the church there may grow significant connections to those who have little to do with the Christian faith. Through communication these people may become more involved in the various elements and activities of the church.[63]

Second, the occasional meeting of networked nodes likely does not provide participants a sufficient amount of time to live in covenant community as a church family. Though Ward explicitly bases the church's existence upon these networked meetings, these meetings do not occur on a regular basis. In such infrequent meetings, would it be possible to live out covenant community? Would it even be possible to determine whether other participants profess Christ or not? Kester Brewin, a UK emerging leader who participates in a liquid church, seems to think so. He has defended the model by stating:

> Church for us then is perhaps simply a network of the infected. Each time two nodes in this network communicate, church is happening, the body is evolving and Christ is being formed. So is there any commitment to one another? Of course. Otherwise the network would collapse. Is there a stress on living like Christ? Of course. It's only when Christlike activity occurs between nodes that synapses are strengthened and the body emerges.[64]

---

62. Ward, *Liquid Church*, 47–48.
63. Ibid.
64. From an interview recorded in Gibbs and Bolger, *Emerging Church*, 114–15.

Assessing Emerging Church Community

However, Brewin seems to have misplaced enthusiasm. A better assessment originates from Michael Moynagh, who cleverly writes that the liquid church structure is so loose that "it may evaporate into gas."[65] Moynagh warns:

> Might relationships be too transient to create real commitment? Gatherings may be too infrequent to build up the body. Fluid encounters with two or three people may be no substitute for the sense of God's presence generated by worshippers together.[66]

Moynagh's warnings resonate with truth, for the liquid model simply does not have enough structure to provide a church with adequate health and accountability.

Church Covenants

Ethic of Love

The New Testament expects that outsiders will know Christ's church for its love.[67] However, in contrast to how many in today's culture define love, the New Testament describes love as involving responsibility, submission, and even humble correction.[68] Because believers deeply love one another, the Scripture expects them to be willing to embrace mutual accountability and gracious correction within the church's life for the glory of God.[69]

---

65. Moynagh, *EmergingChurch.Intro*, 151.

66. Ibid.

67. One thinks of the statement of Jesus in John 13:35, as well as Paul's "one another" admonitions (e.g., Rom 12:10; 13:8; 1 Cor 12:25; Gal 5:13, etc.). Consider also Joseph Hellerman's excellent examination of the type of familial love present in the New Testament's teachings about church life. Hellerman, *When the Church Was a Family*.

68. Regarding loving accountability see: Gal 6:1–4; Titus 3:9–11; 2 Cor 2:5–11. For texts on submission consider: Heb 13:7, 13; 1 Thess 5:12–13; 1 Tim 5:17–18. For texts on corrective church discipline, see: Matt 18:1–8; 1 Cor 5:1–13.

69. Leeman offers helpful insight on this point when he writes, "Theologically, God is not interested merely in relationships. He created humanity

Unfortunately, some leaders within the revisionist stream of the movement conceive of love in a manner foreign to the New Testament. They appear to argue, along with much of contemporary society, that love requires the nonconfrontational acceptance of every lifestyle and behavior. With this line of thinking, they strip Christianity of its doctrinal and ethical demands and reduce the Christian faith down to a simple command to accept others unconditionally.

The work of revisionist leader Peter Rollins serves as a noteworthy example of this mindset. Commenting on 1 John 4:17–16, Rollins writes, "Knowledge of God (the Truth) as a set of propositions is utterly absent; instead he [the writer of 1 John] claims that those who exhibit a genuine love know God, regardless of their religious system."[70] Rollins ignores other themes in John's letter, such as the command to walk in holiness (i.e., the light) or John's concerns for doctrinal purity. Instead, he instructs his readers that all of Christianity consists of the simple feeling of love, and therefore one's beliefs or behavior are nearly irrelevant.[71]

How the Revisionist Ethic of Love Shapes Ecclesiology

This false understanding of love has shaped the ecclesiological practices of some revisionist leaders within the emerging church. For example, Karen Ward once served as a leader (abbess) of Church of the Apostles, an emerging congregation in Seattle,

---

to image and enjoy the pleasure of his glory. Therefore, he calls humanity into a relationship of obedience or conformity to that image. God-to-human and human-to-human relationships should serve that particular end of imaging or worshiping God." Leeman, *Surprising Offense of God's Love*, 138.

70. Rollins, *How (Not) to Speak of God*, 57.

71. DeYoung, with a touch of irony, accuses Rollins at this point of creating a new kind of foundationalism, one that will only accept truth claims that square with his preconceived notion of love. DeYoung writes, "It seems that Rollins has managed to assert a new foundationalism. God is love—that's all we know and everything else is unknown and therefore can only be un/known by the fact that God is love." DeYoung and Kluck, *Why We're Not Emergent*, 125.

Washington. During the time of her leadership, the church had no official doctrinal statement other than the Nicene Creed, and it formulated much of its theology through comments that members posted to a church blog. Explaining her understanding of theology to her church, Ward wrote, "We do not possess truth or seek to correct the truths of others, but we seek to live faithfully in light of the truth of God in Jesus Christ."[72]

Ward's church indeed offered little accountability for its members during the time of her tenure. A listing of the church's "shared values" spoke only to amorphous traits such as "serving our community."[73] Particularly disturbing was the fact that contemporary ethical concerns such as homosexuality received no attention from the church. One frequent attender involved in a homosexual lifestyle stated, "I'm not on the elder board, but since close to COTA's [Church of the Apostles] inception, I've been in so many types of leadership positions and roles, and I'm always challenged. I have the most amazing friendships here, and that's what keeps me in."[74]

---

72. Ward, "Emerging Church and Communal Theology," 179. Revisionist Brian McLaren also seems to allow his false understanding of love to shape his ecclesiology. In a recent chapter on ecclesiology, McLaren emphasizes love within the church to the point that he basically states that love, and love alone, is the true mark of the church. His chapter offers no mention of accountability, restorative discipline, or submission. See McLaren, *New Kind of Christianity*, 161–72.

73. This information was available from the church's website, http://www.apostleschurch.org. See Church of the Apostles, "Church of the Apostles Info."

74. This is the testimony of "James," a faithful COTA member as documented by Tony Jones. See Jones, *New Christians*, 206–7. Revisionist congregations such as Church of the Apostles are correct to speak of love and authenticity. They are also correct in their desire to minister to people not typically associated with the church, such as members of the homosexual community. Here, I have no qualm with the fact that these congregations try to minister to homosexuals; I merely object to the *manner* in which they do so.

Baptists and the Emerging Church Movement

A Baptist Assessment

Historically, many Baptists have argued that a church should use documents such as church covenants and confessions of faith to facilitate the kind of loving accountability envisioned in the New Testament. Confessions of faith are brief summaries of a church's theological beliefs. Jonathan Leeman offers theological justification for a church-wide confession of faith when he writes:

> No verse in the New Testament says, "Churches should have a confession of faith," but the epistles uniformly teach that churches need to hold onto right doctrine and eschew all false doctrine. Though the epistles correct and teach doctrine in their own right, they also speak as if the churches had a shared understanding of the apostle's doctrine (see Gal. 2:2, 7–9).[75]

Similarly, church covenants articulate how the church has agreed to live life together. Having written records of the expected theology and behaviors of church members enables members to better live out biblical covenant commitment with one another, and in the event of failure, it enables the loving enactment of restorative discipline.[76] Because of this, many Baptists have historically understood these two documents to be important tools in the work of creating a regenerate church body.

However, with no shared church covenant or confession of faith, revisionist churches will eventually find themselves unable to preserve any semblance of regenerate membership. The lack of a shared church confession will make it difficult for a church to adjudicate between true and false belief. The absence of a church covenant will mean that church participants who demonstrate no evidence of conversion can easily remain in the church in good standing. It appears, therefore, that Baptists should heed Mark Driscoll's public warning to Karen Ward. Driscoll stated, "Without an awareness of sin, the pursuit of loving community and

---

75. Leeman, *Church and the Surprising Offense of God's Love*, 297.

76. Leeman also offers a persuasive argument for the adoption of a written church covenant. Ibid., 229–70, 299.

nonjudgmental dialogue becomes unprofitable because it is no longer tethered to truth."[77]

Conclusion

The emerging church movement expresses a noble desire to reach postmoderns with the gospel. However, some practices proposed by reconstructionist and, most notably, revisionist leaders have the potential to bring harmful effects upon any church that seeks to enact historic Baptist ecclesiology. Without honest professions of faith, a clearly defined membership, and healthy church structures, emerging church bodies will have no way of protecting regenerate church membership. Baptist church leaders can read emerging church works and receive some profitable insights, such as the emerging church's emphasis on community and the need to allow nonbelievers some degree of involvement. However, Baptists will do well to avoid enacting ecclesiological proposals that might blur their ecclesiological distinctives.

---

77. Driscoll, "Response to Karen Ward," 186.

3

Assessing Emerging Church Worship and Preaching

Dissatisfaction with Contemporary Evangelical Worship

CHRIS ARMSTRONG HAS OBSERVED that many younger evangelicals are "uneasy and alienated in mall-like church environments; high-energy, entertainment-oriented worship; and boomer-era ministry strategies and structures modeled on the business world."[1] Emerging church proposals related to worship stem directly from this dissatisfaction with much of contemporary evangelicalism. Emerging leaders desire to offer relevant worship formats to a generation reared within the postmodern ethos, as they believe that contemporary evangelicalism fails to do so.[2] In this chapter, I will

---

1. Armstrong, "Future Lies in the Past," 26. The fact that many emerging church leaders began their ministry within traditional evangelical churches perhaps demonstrates Armstrong's point.

2. For example, emerging thinker Sally Morgenthaler has criticized modern evangelical worship as being too "focused on human perceptions, needs, feelings, and desires." She argues this approach is out of touch with contemporary American life, explaining that after September 11 "our enforced-happy, you-can-control your world services could no longer maintain the illusion of relevance." Sally Morgenthaler, "Emerging Worship," 222–23. Dan Kimball expresses similar sentiments. Explaining why he wrote his book on emerging worship, Kimball writes, "There is a growing restlessness in many hearts and

Assessing Emerging Church Worship and Preaching

assess popular emerging church proposals related to worship and preaching from a Baptist perspective. As Baptist thought will provide the evaluative tool, I will begin this chapter with a brief overview of several Baptist beliefs related to worship and preaching.

Baptists on Worship and Preaching

While one could certainly write much on public worship in Baptist life, for the sake of brevity I will here only highlight three attributes of Baptist worship relevant for evaluating emerging church proposals. First, Baptists argue that Scripture should have unique authority in shaping a public worship service.[3] Since their inception, Baptists have rejected the notion that non-scriptural sources, such as ecclesiological traditions, equal Scripture in authority. They have therefore endeavored to formulate all of their ecclesiology, including their worship patterns, solely according to Scripture's teaching.[4] The early British Baptists rejected traditions

---

minds... this restless emotional pacing is due to the way most of our churches do not connect and engage with our emerging post-Christian culture. The [traditional] church engages with a modern culture... but most people (especially emerging generations) are living in post-Judeo-Christian times now." Kimball, *Emerging Worship*, x–xi.

3. Consider the Second London Confession's chapter on religious worship. It reads, "The acceptable way of worshipping the true God is instituted by his own revealed will, that he may not be worshipped according to the imaginations and devices of Men, or the suggestions of Satan, under any visible representations, or any other way not prescribed in the Holy Scripture." Second London Confession as recorded in Lumpkin, *Baptist Confessions of Faith*, 280. Similarly, the Baptist pioneer John Smyth spoke of a desire for Scripture, not ecclesiastical traditions, to guide a church's worship when he wrote, "Wee will never be satisfied in endeavoring to reduce the worship and ministry of the Church, to the primitive Apostolique institution from which as yet is so farr distant." Whitley, *Works of John Smyth*, 271. As an aside, by citing the Second London Confession and arguing for the primacy of Scripture in the formulation of the worship service, I am not intending to argue that *all* Baptists have accepted the regulative principle—or that all Baptists should.

4. Baptist theologian R. Stanton Norman has argued, "Baptists, along with other Christian denominations, appeal to the Bible as their ultimate or sole source for religious authority. Baptists distance themselves from other

and practices they perceived as contrary to Scripture and highlighted worship practices commanded in Scripture.[5] Many times this meant that early Baptist worship stood in stark contrast to the accepted Anglican worship of the day, with its strong emphasis upon tradition and ritual. Typical in early Baptist worship were the scripturally mandated practices of prayer, singing (though significant debate over the singing of hymns emerged), preaching, and Scripture reading.[6]

Second, Baptists attempt to emphasize the Scripture during public worship. Early Baptists believed that God employs the Bible as his primary medium for converting sinners. Therefore, they desired to saturate their worship services with Scripture so that the gospel might go forth clearly. In particular, these early Baptists concerned themselves with the preaching act. Neville Clark has described early Baptist worship as "a service of the Word set in the context of prayer and praise"[7] because of the attention the sermon received during the service. Early Baptist confessions specifically mention the preaching act and its necessity.[8] This emphasis upon

---

denominations, however, by claiming a complete dependence upon Scripture as the principle foundation for their beliefs and practices. Whereas certain other Christian groups incorporate extra-biblical sources such as tradition for religious authority, Baptists in their distinctive writings contend that they alone consistently and exclusively hold to the Bible exclusively as their religious authority." Norman, "Southern Baptist Identity," 44–45.

5. Baptists are historically part of the Free Church tradition. Out of a desire to construct their worship solely according to God's Word, Free Church leaders rejected demands from the state that they employ practices they perceived as non-scriptural, such as using the *Book of Common Prayer*. Hughes explains that the designation "free" in the name Free Church "records the desires of both Separatists and Puritans to be free to order corporate worship according to God's Word." Hughes, "Free Church Worship: The Challenge of Freedom," 142–43.

6. See, for example, the list of practices offered in the Second London Confession's article on religious worship. Lumpkin, *Baptist Confessions of Faith*, 280–82.

7. Clark uses this phrase to describe the worship patterns of most nonconforming churches and specifically mentions Baptists as upholding this pattern. Clark, *Call to Worship*, 34.

8. Both the First London Confession and Somerset Confession contain

Scripture and preaching continues among many Baptists today, with contemporary Baptist leader Al Mohler writing, "What do we think preaching is? It is the central act of Christian worship! As a matter of fact, everything else ought to build to the preaching of the Word."[9]

Third, though Baptists share a commitment to the preeminence of Scripture in worship, they have accepted great diversity in the manner in which individual churches carry out the particulars of public worship. Throughout their history, Baptists have accepted different worship styles and patterns as they have attempted to accommodate their worship to various cultures and ministry methodologies. For example, clear distinctions are apparent between the worship patterns of the General Baptists and Particular Baptists in seventeenth-century England.[10] Even the author's own denomination, the Southern Baptist Convention, has a rich heritage of differing worship styles.[11] Presently, Baptist worship is perhaps more diverse than ever, with noted Baptist theologian David Dockery recently cataloguing six different worship styles present within Southern Baptist life alone.[12] Though Baptists would all agree that biblical fidelity requires certain elements in a proper

---

articles that stress the importance of preaching. See Lumpkin, *Baptist Confessions of Faith*, 163, 208.

9 Mohler, "Primacy of Preaching," 9. Another contemporary Baptist thinker who emphasizes the use of Scripture in corporate worship is Jonathan Leeman. See Leeman, *Reverberation*. Also, consider Dever and Alexander, *Deliberate Church*, 77–88.

10. For a good overview, see McKibbens Jr., "Our Baptist Heritage in Worship," 53–69.

11. Two traditions are worthy of brief mention here. The Sandy Creek tradition, originating within revivalism, placed emphasis upon ardor and free expression in worship. By contrast, the Charleston Tradition, epitomized by Olivier Hart of South Carolina, emphasized order and dignity in worship. For an excellent overview of these two traditions, and their influence upon Southern Baptist life today, see Brewer, "Embracing God's Word in Worship," 13–22.

12. Dockery categorizes these styles as: liturgical, traditional, revivalistic, seeker-sensitive/seeker-targeted, praise and worship, and emerging/emergent. Dockery, *Southern Baptist Consensus*, 117–22.

worship service, clearly some freedom exists on how individual churches should best publicly practice these elements.

Emerging Church Worship

Having briefly examined the foundation of Baptist worship practices, I will now consider emerging church worship models. As noted, emerging church proponents desire to offer worship formats relevant to young postmoderns. Therefore, many emerging church worship proposals are inexorably linked to the postmodern ethos. Emerging leaders tend to emphasize four ideals in their worship proposals: experience, participation, the use of ancient worship practices, and an emphasis upon the arts.[13] Here, I will survey and assess some of the more popular emerging worship proposals in each of these four categories. As preaching is such an important component of worship, particularly within the Baptist tradition, a survey and assessment of emerging preaching models will receive individual attention in a subsequent section of this chapter.

Before an examination of emerging worship proposals can begin, however, one brief caveat is needed. As previously noted, Baptists have historically allowed for a rather large amount of diversity in worship to account for different cultural contexts and ministry styles. Therefore, Baptists should not hastily discard emerging worship proposals simply because they are new or different. Baptists should instead seek to assess emerging worship models according to how they will affect Scripture's primacy in a public worship gathering. When assessing emerging proposals, I will concern myself primarily with this issue.

---

13. These four categories are similar to how emerging writer Leonard Sweet has categorized emerging worship. Sweet uses the acronym of EPIC: experiential, participatory, image-driven, and connected. See Sweet, *Post-Modern Pilgrims*.

Experience

The rise of postmodernity has brought about a large epistemological shift in much of the Western world. Postmodern epistemology, in its strongest forms, rejects the value of propositional statements in order to highlight such things as personal experience and authenticity. Emerging church leaders desire to reformulate Christian worship in light of this culture shift. Sally Morgenthaler, for example, writes, "Having shifted from 'knowing-by-notion' to 'knowing-by-narrative,' realignment [worship] in emerging congregations is experiential more than mental, sensory more than read."[14] Morgenthaler argues that emerging worship should engage each of the worshipers' five senses in order to provide a dynamic and engaging worship experience.[15]

Leonard Sweet agrees with Morgenthaler's emphasis upon experience and describes his goal for emerging worship with the acronym EPIC, that is, experiential, participatory, image-rich, and connective. He instructs his readers, "Moderns want to figure out what life's about. Postmoderns what to experience what life is . . . Postmoderns don't want their information straight. They want it laced with experience."[16] To support his argument, Sweet highlights the popularity that Starbucks enjoys among many in the younger generation. He writes, "A cup of coffee [at Starbucks] fetches such a high price because people aren't buying a cup of coffee. They are buying an experience of coffee."[17] Sweet lists several components of this Starbucks experience including such thing as the smell of the coffee and socializing with friends. He sees this as proof that those living during the time of the postmodern transition "don't want staged experiences; they hunger (and thirst) for

---

14. Morgenthaler, "Emerging Worship," 224.

15. Morgenthaler writes that emerging worship should be "visual, aural, tactile, kinetic, emotional, and cerebral." Morgenthaler, "Emerging Worship," 229.

16. Sweet, *Post-Modern Pilgrims*, 33. It is noteworthy that Sweet places experience first in his formulation, as a desire for experience appears to guide the rest of his work.

17. Sweet, *Gospel according to Starbucks*, 32.

Baptists and the Emerging Church Movement

the spontaneity of authentic experience."[18] Sweet believes that the church must embrace worship models that emphasize experience and directly asks his readers, "What's missing, and what can individual Christians and the church at large learn about authentic experience at Starbucks?"[19]

While writers such as Morgenthaler and Sweet tend to deal with this issue of experience more in the abstract, Dan Kimball focuses on offering more practical suggestions for emerging worship. Believing that a fresh approach to worship is "needed in response to our new postmodern culture," Kimball promotes a "multisensory approach comprised of many dimensions and expressions of worship."[20] Like Morgenthaler, Kimball desires for public worship to touch all five physical senses of the worshipers.[21] His church uses pieces of art, video projectors, and even candles in order to offer sights and smells to worshipers. In an attempt to provide audible experiences, Kimball's church encourages the congregation to read creeds and Scripture aloud together. The pastors at Kimball's church even encourage worshipers to move around the sanctuary in order to visit prayer stations in an effort to create tactile experiences during the worship time.[22]

18. Ibid., 37.
19. Ibid., 43.
20. Dan Kimball, *Emerging Worship*, 5, 9.
21. Kimball writes, "Experiential worship brings all five senses into play . . . it tells the story-the good news of the Gospel—with touch, taste, scent, sight, and sound." Kimball and Lewin, *Sacred Space*, 12. One can find Kimball's most substantial defense of this multi-sensory approach in Kimball, *Emerging Church*, 127–31.
22. The prayer stations at Kimball's church feature elements that worshipers can touch. He tells of one service in which the prayer stations featured bowls of water into which worshipers could dip their hands. This was to symbolize their cleanliness before God due to Christ's work on the cross. See Kimball, *Emerging Church*, 168–69. Kimball is certainly not the only emerging leader to advocate using prayer stations as a means of providing sensory experiences. Doug Pagitt writes that worship should be a "full-body participatory experience," and sees prayer stations and the communion meal as important ways to bring about physical experiences in worship. Pagitt, *Church Re-Imagined*, 97–99.

Assessing Emerging Church Worship and Preaching

As Baptists assess this emphasis on experience, both a word of praise and a word of caution are in order. Baptists can praise emerging church leaders for their correct diagnosis of contemporary culture. It is true that the traditional church worship model does not often fit with what many young postmoderns are seeking. Perhaps a renewed emphasis on experience and authenticity in worship will allow churches to connect with younger generations.

However, a word of caution is also appropriate, because problems arise in the way that some emerging leaders go about seeking these worship experiences. Some reconstructionist and revisionist leaders emphasize experience to the point that they appear to minimize or even shun the proclamation of Christian theology. For example, Leonard Sweet writes:

> If the evangelists Matthew, Mark, Luke, or John were here, they would tell you that faith is not primarily a matter of belief. They would emphasize instead aspects of life that are closer to what we would call passion. They would describe faith as immersion and engagement, a full-on experience of life that is far bigger than everyday experience.[23]

Elsewhere, Sweet appears to tell his readers to assess their church primarily on its ability to engender beautiful experiences during worship, not on its doctrinal convictions. He writes, "Don't focus on what it [the reader's church] believes or its official statement of faith; rather, consider how much time your church expends in creating beauty. What does it do to develop embodied practices and multisensory experiences?"[24]

---

23. Sweet, *Gospel according to Starbucks*, 17.

24. Ibid., 56. Sweet is certainly not alone in this trend. McLaren devotes an entire chapter in *A Generous Orthodoxy* to minimizing the importance of theology in an effort to emphasize the beauty of mystical experiences. See McLaren, *Generous Orthodoxy*, 161–75. In addition, when describing their worship practices, congregants at Church of the Apostles write, "We are a bit weary of words . . . instead, we are looking for nonpropositional ways of coming to understand the atonement, ways that involve art, ritual, community, etc." See Ward, "Emerging Church and Communal Theology," 163–64. Interestingly, DeYoung accuses the more radical elements of the emerging movement, with

Statements such as these reveal that some emerging church proponents have become too accepting of our culture's obsession with the existential and the subjective. It is certainly not a sin for worshippers to desire a sense of transcendence in a worship gathering. However, worship models that emphasize existential experience and shun theological reflection should concern Baptists, because Baptists have historically emphasized the primacy of the Word in worship gatherings. Though not a Baptist, David Wells offered a critique of some emerging church leaders that Baptists can agree with when he wrote, "Those churches that have banished pulpits or are 'getting beyond' the truth question are going beyond Christianity itself... images we may want, entertainment we may desire, but it is the proclamation of Christ crucified and risen that is the church's truth to tell."[25]

Participation

Emerging leaders also value opportunities for participation in worship. Frequently in emerging church literature, writers group the ideals of experience and participation together, because they argue that allowing worshipers to participate will improve the worship experience.

Dan Kimball's worship model certainly places a high value upon participation. He advocates such things as moving the worship band to the side (or even to the back) of the church so that it does not take precedence over the worshipers.[26] In addition, instead of having a pre-determined order of service, his church will

---

their emphasis upon experience over doctrine, of simply rehashing the old Protestant liberalism of Schleiermacher or Fosdick. See DeYoung and Kluck, *Why We're Not Emergent*, 114–17.

25. Wells, *Courage to Be Protestant*, 207.

26. One can find a description in Kimball, *Emerging Church*, 137–38. Elsewhere Kimball states, "The room is set up to have everyone looking up at the screens and not the music band; the music leaders are off to the side, so that they aren't coming across like a rock concert. They're not the focal point, though we still do music." Preaching Magazine, "Preaching in the Emerging Church," 9.

Assessing Emerging Church Worship and Preaching

sometimes allow congregants to spontaneously select the songs the church will sing.[27] Kimball hopes that such steps will allow worshipers to feel they are actively worshiping Christ instead of merely viewing a concert. He explains that his goal is to move his church "past merely listening and singing to a whole new level of ways to participate in the worship service."[28]

Revisionist leaders also speak of the need for greater participation in worship. Karen Ward, the former leader of Church of the Apostles, contrasted the worship in her church with worship in the traditional church by stating, "For the most part, we have no up-front leader, no stage, no presiding priest, no big pastor."[29] Under her leadership, the church sought "multigenerational and highly participatory."[30] Ward described a service at her church by writing, "On one Sunday, we finger painted. We made a cloth altar, and everyone put their painted hand on the cloth. This is like 'godly play,' like Montessori church."[31]

Other revisionist leaders have spoken of churches with an open microphone policy, church meetings with no predetermined plan or pattern, and church policies that encourage radical transparency and openness on the part of the worshipers during the service.[32] Revisionist Doug Pagitt has even attempted to recon-

---

27. Kimball, "Emerging Worship," 312.

28. Kimball, *Emerging Worship*, 81–82.

29. Gibbs and Bolger believe that "participating as producers" is a key theme of the entire emerging movement and they dedicate an entire chapter in their book to this concept. Gibbs and Bolger, *Emerging Churches*, 155ff. Karen Ward's statements are from an interview recorded in Gibbs and Bolger. See Gibbs and Bolger, *Emerging Churches*, 164–65.

30. Ibid.

31. Ibid., 165.

32. The Sanctuary, an emerging gathering in California, employs an open microphone policy. This church meets in a dance club and offers a public question and answer time to those who attend. Jonny Baker, part of Grace Church in London, discourages a pre-determined worship order in order to create flexibility in the worship schedule. Kester Brewin's church, entitled Vaux, seeks to encourage a radical openness during the public worship time. Brewin compares this model of transparency to contributor-powered websites such as Slashdot.com. For these examples and others, see Gibbs and Bolger, 164–69.

figure traditional church furniture patterns out of a desire to create intimacy and participation. Pagitt explains that he moved his church furniture into the shape of a circle "because our gatherings are designed to be interactive and participatory."[33]

Baptists will certainly appreciate a desire for more congregational participation in worship. After all, their model of congregational polity encourages participation from the church body in matters of church governance. For this reason, emerging church leaders deserve a wide readership from Baptist leaders.

However, some of the proposals that originate within the revisionist stream of the emerging church movement might distract a congregation from clearly hearing the Scripture, a possibility that should concern Baptists.[34] One must question the possibility of meditating on the preached Word in a service that calls on worshipers to participate in a number of activities concurrently.[35] As each worshiper acts in a way that maximizes his or her own spiritual experiences, clearly some attenders will distract others, even if they do so unintentionally. Critics from the traditional church are therefore perhaps correct to accuse some revisionist worship services of missing "simplicity, directness, and sparseness—and in directly theological terms, a Christocentric, Good News-atonement-repentance-pressing-on model, with the Word as the leading evangel."[36]

Ancient Worship Practices

Sally Morgenthaler has written that emerging worship "is wholesale deconstruction—the dismantling of a multiplicity of worship

---

33. Pagitt, *Church Re-Imagined*, 65.

34. One cannot be dogmatic on this point, and I only offer this criticism as a friendly warning to these leaders.

35. Morgenthaler describes a revisionist worship service well when she writes, "The order of service may be more concurrent (several things happening at once) than homogeneous (everyone doing the same things at the same time)." Morgenthaler, "Emerging Worship," 226.

36. Best, "Emerging Worship," 235.

Assessing Emerging Church Worship and Preaching

forms (both pre-Reformation and post-Reformation) followed by the postmodern art of pastiche: creating something unprecedented out of the pieces at hand."[37] Following the style of postmodern artists, some emerging church leaders attempt to bring worship styles and practices from different eras in church history together into one service. Of particular interest to these leaders are the so-called ancient worship practices.[38]

Emerging worship gatherings can feature such ancient practices as prayer labyrinths, prayer stations, and the use of icons. Prayer labyrinths are large pathways designed for walking that feature a winding, circuitous route to a center point. The creators of the labyrinths intend them to be metaphors of the Christian life as "we progress down a path that's laid out by God-even though we rarely foresee its twists and turns—toward the eventual goal of unity with Christ."[39] Prayer stations offer prepared sites where worshipers can stop and contemplate the transcendent.[40] Emerging leaders have adopted the use of icons from Eastern forms of Christianity because "we live in an image-saturated world" and this practice helps us to "take seriously our image-based lives."[41] Following the postmodern ethos, emerging leaders will typically

---

37. Morgenthaler, "Emerging Worship," 225. Morgenthaler is correct to tie this aspect of emerging church worship to postmodern artistic sensibilities. Postmodernity, with its denial of metanarratives, refuses "to give a work of art any coherent overall design." Instead, postmodern artists "favor the pastiche or collage—a patchwork of disconnected images that defy any attempt at interpretation." See Pearcey, *Saving Leonardo*, 238.

38. Though emerging authors frequently use the phrase "ancient" worship practices, many times they are actually referring to practices prevalent in medieval Christianity, not practices found in the early church. Throughout this chapter I will use the term ancient, however, as this is the term emerging leaders seem to prefer when describing their model. See Haykin's brief critique concerning this point. Haykin, review of *Finding Our Way Again*, 66.

39. Jones, *Sacred Way*, 131. Kimball advocates the use of prayer labyrinths in Kimball, *Emerging Church*, 168–69.

40. For emerging church descriptions of the use of prayer stations, see Kimball, *Emerging Church*, 165–68; Jones, *Sacred Way*, 135–47; and Pagitt, *Church Re-Imagined*, 97–99.

41. Jones, *Sacred Way*, 104.

place these ancient practices into a worship meeting that also features modern technologies and contemporary music styles.

Emerging leaders who advocate for these practices believe that their inclusion offers a worship format meaningful to postmoderns. In the introductory volume to a new emerging church series on worship, McLaren writes that a return of these practices would offer a healthy alternative to "militaristic scientific secularism, pushy religious fundamentalism, and mushy amorphous spirituality."[42] For his part, Kimball also promotes a return to ancient worship practices out of the belief that they will benefit postmodern seekers. Kimball argues that much of contemporary evangelical worship is shallow and beholden to modernity, while a return to ancient practices will offer curious postmoderns the sense of transcendence and connectedness to the past that they are seeking.[43]

Not only does Kimball encourage the use of these practices, he even attempts to decorate his church's worship space with artifacts that give a sense of antiquity. His church places candles and stained glass windows throughout the worship area and even projects images of the interiors of gothic cathedrals on the building's walls.[44] His church engages in these practices with the intention of providing a feeling of the ancient and transcendent.

In assessing the emerging church's fascination with ancient worship practices, Baptists should begin by immediately rejecting worship practices that are observed in a manner that distorts or minimizes the gospel. For this reason, the manner in which at least one emerging church revisionist desires to return to ancient worship practices should trouble Baptists. In *Finding Our Way Again*, not once does Brian McLaren connect the observance of

42. McLaren, *Finding Our Way Again*, 4.

43. He instructs his readers, "Take time to learn the history of various expressions of worship . . . there is a richness to be found in looking back in church history and implementing ancient forms of worship, in addition to more recent ways." Kimball, "Emerging Worship," 10.

44. Kimball sometimes refers to his worship methodology as "vintage worship." He devotes an entire chapter of his book to instructing readers on how to create "vintage worship spaces." Kimball, *Emerging Church*, 133–42.

ancient worship practices with the message of the gospel. In this work, McLaren speaks of the need for inner purging, serious contemplation over sin, and lifestyle modification, but he fails to adequately explain how a person can accomplish such things apart from a robust meditation upon the freedom found in the gospel.[45] The fact that McLaren wishes to include practices from the three major world religions—Islam, Judaism, and Christianity—and not simply those that are exclusive to the Christian faith, further compounds the problem. Ultimately, it appears that McLaren, despite his protests to the contrary, seeks to incorporate these practices merely to accommodate postmodernity's desire for gospel-less "spirituality."[46]

Theologically conservative leaders who employ the use of these practices fare better. Kimball's use of ancient worship practices to create a sense of transcendence in the worship space does not in and of itself lead to a minimization of the gospel.[47] In fact, Kimball's approach could even offer a corrective to much of contemporary evangelical worship, which is many times devoid of any sense of the transcendent.

---

45. This becomes especially apparent in the concluding chapters of McLaren's *Finding Our Way Again*. There, McLaren instructs readers to purge sin from their lives ("via purgative") and to meditate upon God's truth ("via illuminative"). McLaren, however, unfortunately fails to mention the gospel in these chapters and, rather tellingly, also rarely mentions God's revelation found in Scripture. See McLaren, *Finding Our Way Again*, 151–81.

46. Carson wonderfully documents and analyzes postmodern culture's obsession with spiritual experiences apart from the gospel. See Carson, *Gagging of God*, 555–69.

47. One must remember that Kimball does not advocate using *only* practices such as labyrinths and prayer stations in worship. He does argue for the necessity of the preached Word and discusses the need for preaching at length (this fact will be examined below). Therefore, the ancient practices in Kimball's service are meant to accompany, not replace, gospel preaching and singing. The author here is merely stating that these practices, when done in the context of meditation upon the preached gospel, may be profitable and interesting to younger generations.

Baptists and the Emerging Church Movement

Emphasis upon the Arts

The emerging movement argues that modern evangelicalism, because of an uncritical acceptance of modernity, has too often espoused a dualism that separates sacred and secular as well as physical and spiritual.[48] In response to this trend, emerging leaders desire to promote holistic worship, that is, worship intended to encompass all areas of one's life. They desire for worship to consist not simply of a service that takes place one day of the week. Instead, they insist that Christian worship should occur daily and in all aspects of one's personhood, including one's work, leisure, and relationships.

Emerging leaders involved in this discussion have expressed particular concern over the neglect of the arts in worship. They believe that modernity's dualism has caused evangelical worship to focus so extensively on the intellect that it has neglected the physical and the creative. Pagitt seeks to offer a corrective when he writes, "Our creativity comes from a desire to live life as people who are created in the image of a creative God, who are invited to be co-(re)creators with God."[49] Because God designed humans with a propensity for creativity, Pagitt argues we should embrace artistic expression in worship as a means of giving praise back to God. He explains, "The Gospel is packed with the implication that we have something to give because of our redemption. We are told to go, to make, to build, to speak, to touch, to feed, to create."[50] By involving the entire person, the creative as well as the rational, Pagitt hopes to foster holistic worship. His church seeks to offer a refuge for artists and outlets for the creative, sometimes even during the worship service.

---

48. Gibbs and Bolger note that the desire to become holistic worshipers and breach the supposed sacred/secular divide is a key thought in emerging churches. Gibbs and Bolger, *Emerging Churches*, 65–88. McLaren also accuses contemporary evangelicalism of succumbing to the sort of dualistic thinking mentioned here. McLaren, "Everything Old Is New Again," 23–25.

49. Pagitt, *Church Re-Imagined*, 183.

50. Ibid., 185.

Assessing Emerging Church Worship and Preaching

While many emerging writers agree with Pagitt's conclusions, Peter Rollins is worthy of special mention.[51] Originating from revisionist stream of the movement, Rollins argues that the emerging movement is moving to embrace a form of art he entitles transformance art.[52] Rollins explains the purpose of transformance art is not only to offer creative praise to God but to also elicit a worldview change in the minds of the worshipers. He believes that all aspects of the worship gathering, not just the preaching, can enact spiritual and psychological change upon the worshipers and hence this emphasis upon art in worship. Pagitt actually appears to argue for something similar to Rollins on this point, though he does not use the phrase transformance art, when he speaks of using art pieces as a "sermon" in his church.[53]

When assessing these proposals, Baptists should exercise enough humility to admit that certain emerging church critiques of traditional church worship appear correct. Some traditional churches do appear to present worship as only a service that occurs on Sunday morning instead of an undertaking that encompasses all of one's life. Emerging leaders, on this point, correctly remind the church that Christianity has no room for gnostic thinking or a lack of concern with life in the here and now. Churches should instruct members how to worship God with all of their being, including their artistic giftedness.[54]

---

51. Many emerging leaders have expressed sentiments similar to Pagitt's. Even Mark Driscoll, a member of the relevant stream of the movement, highlights the importance of the arts. He explains, "In our city [Seattle], great value is placed upon creativity and the arts. In our kingdom culture, we also hold these things in high regard and believe that one of God's attributes is beauty." Driscoll goes on to explain how his church displays "paintings, photos, and works in other media for the sake of beauty and the encouragement of the artists." Driscoll, *Radical Reformission*, 186.

52. Rollins, "Transformance Art," 98.

53. Pagitt, *Preaching Re-Imagined*, 186–87.

54. Liederbach and Reid attempt to combine the positive elements of the emerging church model and the traditional church model into a proposal they entitle convergent church. Concerning convergent church worship they helpfully write, "By recognizing that every act, every deed, every word, every meal, everything I do was meant to be an act of worship, each of these acts presents

While agreeing with emerging leaders that worship should involve all aspects of one's life, Baptists should also carefully uphold the preeminence of Scripture in a public worship service. Baptists rightly understand the Scriptures to be the primary source of moral and spiritual transformation. This fact means that in public worship the Scriptures should receive chief attention, because they alone have the power to convert.[55] Pieces of artwork and other forms of artistic expression certainly have value and can even edify a church's corporate worship time. Yet, these things should not take precedence over a church's attention to the Scriptures.

It is here that revisionists such as Rollins and Pagitt seem to err. Pagitt incorrectly labels an artistic exhibit put on by his church a sermon, and even implies that such a thing has equal value to the preached Word.[56] For his part, Rollins emphasizes the role of art in personal transformation but gives no mention of Scripture and its power to change.[57] While Baptists can commend these leaders for their artistic sensibilities and their desire for holistic worship, Baptists should also caution these leaders that churches that seek true transformation should make the Scriptures their focal point.

Emerging Church Preaching

As previously noted, Baptists have historically emphasized the importance of the preaching act in their worship services. Therefore, it is appropriate to give particular attention to emerging proposals related to preaching. The emerging church movement, a collection of individuals and churches that have divergent views on theology and methodology, contains several different homiletical models.

---

an occasion for worship. Through the Gospel of Jesus Christ, the most mundane aspects of life are transformed from mundane details to opportunities to glorify God." Liederbach and Reid, *Convergent Church*, 126.

55. Mohler warns, "To replace the expository preaching of God's Word with anything else at all is to abandon the means God has determined to use to call his people to Himself." Mohler, *He Is Not Silent*, 61.

56. Pagitt, *Preaching Re-Imagined*, 186–87.

57. Rollins, "Transformance Art," 89–102.

Assessing Emerging Church Worship and Preaching

However, for the sake of brevity, I will give attention here to only two popular emerging church preaching models.[58]

Doug Pagitt's Progressional Dialogue

The revisionist leader Doug Pagitt proposes a complete restructuring of the preaching act in order to accommodate postmodern listeners. He believes that the traditional church has incorrectly equated preaching with "speaching." Pagitt himself coined the term speaching and he defines it as, "The style of preaching that's hardly distinguishable from a one-way speech."[59] Here, Pagitt has in mind the typical sermon in most traditional churches, in which one man speaks while the attenders listen in silence. Believing this speaching style of preaching to be a product of modernity, Pagitt deems it an ineffective and perhaps even immoral way of communicating in today's postmodern world. He decries speaching as "an ineffectual means of communication" that "damages our people and creates a sense of powerlessness in them."[60] With extreme hyperbole, Pagitt even argues that regular speaching "may well be an act of relational violence, one that is detrimental to the very communities we are seeking to nurture."[61]

To combat the perceived failures of speaching, Pagitt proposes a model he entitles progressional dialogue. In this model, "the context of the presentation is established in the context of a healthy relationship between the presenter and the listeners, and substantive changes in the context are then created as a result of

---

58. While other models are perhaps worthy of treatment, for the sake of brevity I have decided to survey and assess only two popular emerging leaders and their preaching models. I have chosen these two leaders because: (1) they represent different streams of the emerging movement and therefore display the movement's diversity; (2) they have written extensively on homiletics and offer unique contributions to the field; and (3) their models have generated much interest.

59. Pagitt, *Preaching Re-Imagined*, 11–12.

60. Ibid., 22.

61. Ibid., 26.

this relationship."[62] The progressional dialogue model encourages members of a church community to participate during the preaching act in order to complete the sermon in conjunction with the preacher. Pagitt believes this form of dialogue will allow attenders to view themselves as participants in the sermon as well as in the story of God.

Pagitt cites his preaching work at Solomon's Porch, the church he attends, as an example of how one can employ the progressional dialogue model. During the week at his church, a Bible discussion group will meet with in order to collectively craft the sermon.[63] Then, as the message is delivered on Sunday morning, Pagitt "invites others to share their ideas, input, and thoughts about what's been said."[64] Pagitt makes it his primary goal during this preaching time to not convey information to the worshipers but to instead encourage openness and transparency. Pagitt even intends the seating arrangements at his church to encourage participation. Worshipers at this church sit in a circle in order to give the preaching time the feeling of a roundtable discussion.[65]

Pagitt gives little biblical support for his position. However, he does offer a theological argument that should interest Baptists. He states that the doctrine of the priesthood of all believers favors his model, not the speaching model, and he bases much of his theological support upon this point.[66]

In response, Baptists might say that Scripture indeed calls all believers to edify one another with the Word during the worship service (e.g., Col 3:16). However, Paul also envisions an orderly Christian worship gathering in which one person at a time speaks while the others remain silent. Paul encourages this so that the

   62. Ibid., 23.
   63. Pagitt, *Preaching Reimagined*, 107.
   64. Ibid., 24.
   65. Ibid., 207.
   66. Pagitt offers no significant exegesis of any biblical text, though he does cite Acts 10 as a potential example of progressional dialogue. Concerning the priesthood of all believers, Pagitt explains, "A belief in the priesthood of all believers compels us to reconsider our ideas about speaching and pastoral authority." Ibid., 152–53.

Assessing Emerging Church Worship and Preaching

church might present the Word in a non-distracting manner.[67] For reasons such as this one, Baptists, while they certainly believe in the priesthood of all believers, have historically not understood the doctrine of the priesthood of all believers to require anything akin to the progressional dialogue model.

For another reason Pagitt's model should arouse concern among Baptists. As noted in the previous chapter, Baptists have historically placed a high value on preserving a regenerate church body. However, Pagitt so strongly desires to welcome differing views that he freely welcomes unbelievers to participate in the sermon through the progressional dialogue process. He writes:

> We listen to unbelievers on everything from the way we spend our money and how we educate our children to the way we care for our bodies and how we interact with the environment. So when the church maintains practices that silence the unbeliever, we reinforce the idea that preaching is intended for the safety of the church, not to help us connect with the full spectrum of our lives.[68]

Clearly, a model that advocates allowing those who are unregenerate to preach during the sermon time in order to "connect with the full spectrum of our lives" should discomfort Baptists, who argue that these unbelievers have no place as members, much less preachers within the church body.

Pagitt's proposals ultimately stem from a rather dangerous view concerning the nature of community and truth. The Scripture in Pagitt's model is merely "*an* authoritative member of the community."[69] In a complete capitulation to radical postmodernity, Pagitt gives final authority to the community that seeks to understand the Scripture. His model welcomes divergent views on the nature of God and insists upon their acceptance because

---

67. See 1 Cor 14:26–33. Paul states that he gives this instruction so that "everyone may learn and everyone may be encouraged" (Holman Christian Standard Bible).

68. Pagitt, *Preaching Re-Imagined*, 224.

69. Ibid., 31, emphasis added. Note that the Bible is *an* authoritative member but not *the* authoritative member.

one's personal testimony about God "should be listened to with the same sense of respect and reverence as the Bible itself."[70] Richard Holland rightly notes that in Pagitt's proposal "subjective experience is promoted to divine fiat while Scripture is demoted to community member. The pews become pulpits as the Bible is escorted to take a seat in a pew."[71]

Dan Kimball's Theotopical Preaching Model and Call for Humility

Emerging church relevant Dan Kimball also offers a preaching model worthy of attention. Kimball cites Paul's ministry to Jews and Gentiles in Acts 17:16–34 as an example of how pastors should adjust their preaching in order to accommodate a particular audience's worldview. Noting that Paul addressed the Jews of Thessalonica differently from how he addressed the pagans of Athens, Kimball writes, "Paul used two different starting points for two different audiences, based on their worldview and knowledge of Scripture."[72] Kimball argues that, in the spirit of Paul, pastors today must now retool their homiletical models in order to accommodate the rise of postmodernity. His preaching model attempts to do just that, first, by placing an emphasis on preaching the grand narrative of the Scripture and second, by emphasizing humility and authenticity.

Kimball makes conveying the grand narrative of the biblical story a prominent part of his preaching model because, much like Paul's audience at Athens, today's postmodern listeners likely lack

---

70. Ibid., 218–19. Elsewhere Pagitt writes, "Because each of us has a personal relationship with God, it makes sense that each of us would have a personal understanding of God." Ibid., 125.

71. Holland, "Progressional Dialogue and Preaching," 215. Another statement worthy of mention comes from David Wells. Wells writes, "Preaching is not a conversation, a chat about some interesting ideas. It is not the moment in which postmoderns hear their own private message in the biblical words, one unique to each one who hears, and then go their own way. No! This is *God* speaking!" Wells, *Courage to Be Protestant*, 230.

72. Kimball, *Emerging Church*, 176.

Assessing Emerging Church Worship and Preaching

familiarity with the major storyline of the biblical text. He calls upon preachers to "become storytellers again"[73] and describes his goal for a sermon by writing, "What I try to do, in a narrative sense, is to be constantly piecing in where what we're talking about fits with the grand narrative of the biblical story."[74]

Out of this desire to convey Scripture's grand metanarrative in a sermon, Kimball promotes a model entitled theotopical preaching. The term theotopical, coined by Kimball himself, shows an attempt to wed expository preaching and topical preaching together. Kimball's theotopical messages typically feature verse-by-verse explanation, as expository messages typically do. However, he also structures his sermons around a central theological theme, as is sometimes the case in topical messages. He describes his model by writing:

> We should be expository in terms of doing the right exegetical work for biblically rooted messages. But at the same time preaching is an opportunity to shape a theological worldview for people by telling the story. Every time I preach I clearly know what theological concept I am trying to teach and how it fits into the story of the Bible.[75]

Kimball offers one of his sermons on dating as an example of theotopical preaching. He explains that, while he was teaching on sanctification in a dating relationship, he also made a point of focusing the message around the doctrine of creation and God's creation of male and female in Genesis.[76]

The second component of Kimball's preaching model is a call for the preacher to exhibit humility and authenticity. Kimball warns his readers "there will be a great backlash from emerging generations if they sense loftiness or arrogance" because "people in emerging generations look at our hearts more than at the words

---

73. Ibid.
74. Preaching, "Preaching in the Emerging Church," 51.
75. Kimball, *Emerging Church*, 180.
76. Ibid.

we speak."⁷⁷ Kimball attempts to model humility to his readers by publicly dedicating each sermon to the Lord in order to prevent the sin of pride.⁷⁸ Kimball's call for pastoral humility goes beyond a pastor's internal disposition, however. He also calls for pastors to exercise humility in their interpretation of Scripture and reacts rather strongly to the certainty with which some pastors espouse their theological convictions.⁷⁹ Though Kimball remains within the bounds of theological orthodoxy, he argues that pastors ministering in today's postmodern world should carefully demonstrate a hermeneutic of humility.⁸⁰

When surveying Kimball's proposals from a Baptist perspective, I believe that most Baptists will have no major concerns with his theotopical preaching model. With his model, Kimball merely attempts to offer a verse-by-verse exposition while simultaneously exposing his congregation to some of the grand theological themes in Scripture. Most Baptists, especially after considering Pagitt's model, will doubtlessly find Kimball's concern for exposition and theology refreshing. Some Baptists might object that Kimball's theotopical model has the potential to allow the sermon topic, rather than the text, to be the primary shaper of the message. While this concern has some legitimacy, I view this to be a minor objection and do not view Kimball's proposal as so offensive that Baptists must completely reject it.

Regarding Kimball's calls for hermeneutical and personal humility on the part of the one preaching, at least one Baptist pastor

---

77. Ibid., 195.

78. Kimball reports that before he preaches he typically lifts his hands into the air and prays something along the lines of, "Lord, I surrender everything to you. I cannot do this without you. May your Spirit speak through me. Your will, not mine. I can not do this without you, please speak through me." Ibid., 196.

79. For example, Kimball tells of his background in a fundamentalist, dispensationalist church. He reacts negatively to his upbringing and bemoans the fact that so many Christians are satisfied with "wrapped-up, tidy, black-and-white answers" while the issues are in fact typically "far more complex." Kimball, "Emerging Church and Missional Theology," 90.

80. See in particular Kimball, "Humble Theology," 214–24.

has expressed concern that perhaps Kimball goes too far. John Bohannon warns, "In an attempt to contextualize the message to a postmodern culture, in hopes that non-Christians might come to love Jesus and like the church, Kimball's non-confrontational homiletic might just inadvertently be itching [sic] the ears of those he is trying to reach."[81] In particular, Bohannon points to several statements Kimball makes in his *They Like Jesus but Not the Church*.[82] Yet, Kimball holds to conservative evangelical theology and merely desires to eliminate some of the arrogance found in the church's past, not shy away from the proclamation of Christian truth. In a postmodern culture so suspicious of strong leadership, Kimball's model of homiletical humility will probably prove very profitable. Bohannon rightly believes that a preacher must not shirk from his responsibility to proclaim the Word, yet perhaps his criticism is more appropriate for those within the revisionist stream of the emerging movement.

Conclusion

Baptists can praise the emerging church movement for accurately understanding the cultural milieu in which we minister. Baptists can also stand to learn from some of the movement's thoughtful critiques of contemporary evangelical worship. However, Baptists should never seek to trade Scripture's primacy in worship for some

---

81. Bohannon, "Preaching and the Emerging Church," 310. Bohannon presently serves as pastor of Water's Edge Community Church, a Baptist congregation in Clarksville, Virginia.

82. Of particular concern for Bohannon is the fact that Kimball nearly appears to apologize for biblical teachings that might be controversial in today's society. For example, though Kimball holds to a conservative position on homosexuality, he states, "I don't take the issue lightly or without compassion for those who might be hurt by hearing my position." Kimball, *They Like Jesus but Not the Church*, 138. Bohannon responds to this statement by writing, "Is this a postmodern or emergent homiletical phenomenon to equate truth that frees people from bondage and sin with hurting people? If a preacher's homiletical philosophy begins to incorporate the view that proclaiming the truth actually hurts people, will it be long before that preacher stops sharing truth or changes his message?" Bohannon, "Preaching and the Emerging Church," 310n94.

of the misguided attempts at cultural relevance found among some revisionist and reconstructionist leaders. Doing so may minimize God's means of bringing about conversion and spiritual maturity.

4

Assessing Emerging Church Missional Ministry

Seeking a Missional Church

WHILE THE WESTERN WORLD was moving from modernity to postmodernity in the late twentieth century, another cultural shift was also taking place. The influence of Christianity, for so long an important part of Western culture and society, experienced a precipitous decline. Today, the Christian worldview no longer enjoys the cultural primacy it once did in the West. This is particularly true in nations historically linked to Christianity, such as those in Western Europe. Cultural observers, including many emerging writers, have described this removal of Christian influence as "the end of Christendom."[1]

It was not long until Christian missiologists began to take note of this trend. For such thinkers, the Western world, the traditional sending base for world missions, had now become a mission field. Leaders such as Lesslie Newbigin and Darrell Guder called on the Western church to view itself no longer as an institution but as a collection of missionaries serving God in a non-Christian

1. Driscoll, *Religion Saves*, 211; Murray, *Post-Christendom*. See also Gibbs and Bolger, *Emerging Churches*, 17–18.

society.² They popularized the term missional to describe this understanding of the church. Guder, for example, writes, "With the term missional, we emphasize the essential nature and vocation of the church as God's called and sent people."³

While the works of Newbigin and Guder have influenced many Western Christians, they have especially captured the attention of emerging church leaders.⁴ Emerging leaders desire for the church to effectively minister in the postmodern, post-Christian Western world, and they view the missional church paradigm as a means of accomplishing this goal.⁵ They have written extensively on what it means for a church to serve missionally in our cultural context.

In this chapter, after a brief overview of Baptist thought on these issues, I will survey popular emerging church proposals intended to create a missional church. I will then assess these proposals from a Baptistic understanding of the church. Because of the incredible diversity of the emerging movement, not all emerging leaders agree on what a missional church should specifically look like. Therefore, I will consider emerging church proposals

---

2. See, for example, Newbigin, *Open Secret*; Guder, *Missional Church*; Guder, *Continuing Conversion of the Church*. Consider also Bosch, *Transforming Mission*.

3. Guder, "Missional Church," 11. Jonathan Leeman documents Guder's responsibility for the popularity of the term missional in Jonathan Leeman, "What Is the Missional Church?"

4. When reading emerging church literature that discusses the church's mission, one cannot help but to notice the emerging movement's indebtedness to Newbigin and Guder. Here are but a few examples of emerging citing these authors: Anderson, *Emergent Theology*, 178–80; McLaren, *Generous Orthodoxy*, 120–21, 255–56; Kimball, *Emerging Church*, 68–70. Mark Driscoll even explicitly connects the beginning of the emerging church movement with the influence of Guder, Newbigin, and the Gospel and Our Culture Network in Driscoll and Breshears, *Vintage Church*, 218–19.

5. There has been such overlap between the missional church discussion and the emerging church discussion that some leaders, such as Mark Driscoll, have declared the terms to be practically synonymous. See Driscoll, *Religion Saves*, 210. See also Driscoll, *Radical Reformission*, 17–18. For further treatment of the relationship between missional movement and emerging movement, see the first chapter of this project.

individually. I will begin by examining Mark Driscoll's understanding of the term missional and will later examine how leaders within the revisionist stream of the emerging movement define the term. Driscoll uses the term missional to describe such things as engaging non-Christians where they live, contextualizing the gospel and church life to fit our present culture, and using the multisite church model to reach large numbers of people. Revisionist leaders use the term missional to call the church to usher in God's kingdom through involvement in such actions as social work.

Baptists and Missional

Mark Driscoll employs the multisite model in an attempt to missionally reach more people. As I will demonstrate, Driscoll's particular use of the multisite model raises questions related to local church autonomy. Historically, most Baptists have advocated for a form of congregational polity in which the local congregation governs itself under the Christ's lordship. R. Stanton Norman explains that this model of polity "emphasizes the autonomy, independence, and authority of the local church."[6] While Baptists believe in cooperation between congregations, they shun ecclesiological models in which entities outside of the local church make authoritative decisions for the church. I will assess Driscoll's use of the multisite model according to this historic Baptist conviction.

Historic Baptist thought offers little information in regards to how revisionists employ the term missional.[7] However, in their works on missional ministry, some revisionist leaders do mention such theological concepts as the gospel and the expansion of the kingdom of God. Baptist theologians have certainly spoken on these issues. I will assess how revisionist leaders understand the gospel and the kingdom of God in light what Baptist theologians

---

6. Norman, *Baptist Way*, 86.

7. The particular manner in which modern missional proponents discuss contextualization and missional living is rather new. Historic Baptist thought provides little related to this discussion.

such as George Eldon Ladd and Russell Moore have written on these topics.

Mark Driscoll and the Meaning of Missional

Mark Driscoll claims the adjective missional as a signature mark of his theology, and he frequently uses phrases such as "missional, reformed, charismatic" or "reformissional" to describe his approach to ministry.[8] A survey of his work reveals that his missional engagement occurs on three main fronts. First, following the lead of thinkers such as Newbigin, he desires for members of the Western church to view themselves as missionaries operating within a non-Christian culture. Second, he desires to contextualize the gospel message and church life so that they might be understandable to people living in the post-Christian West. Third, he employs the multisite church model in an effort to reach large numbers of people.

Driscoll on Missional Living

Driscoll calls upon the church to engage the post-Christian West as missionaries when he writes, "Reformission is a radical call to reform the church's traditionally flawed view of missions as something carried out only in foreign lands and to focus instead on the urgent need in our own neighborhoods."[9] For Driscoll, this fact primarily means that Christians must have the courage and freedom to engage nonbelievers where they work and play. To illustrate this point, he speaks of Christians who work as rock band managers, beer brewers, and tattoo artists in order to engage the lost.[10]

---

8. For "reformed, charismatic, missional," see Driscoll, *Religion Saves*, 216. Driscoll also employs the term reformissional to describe his intentions, attempting to convey the combination of the missional movement with his soteriological convictions. See Driscoll, *Radical Reformission*; Driscoll, *Religion Saves*, 210.

9. Driscoll, *Radical Reformission*, 18.

10. Ibid. Stories such as these are interspersed between the chapters in

He instructs his readers to "dance as close to sinners as possible by crossing lines that unnecessarily separate the people God has found from those he is still seeking." By doing so, he tells his readers they will be "living freely within the culture as missionaries."[11]

Driscoll, then, represents a rather unique blend of theological conservatism and cultural engagement. His theology offers no departure from the historic doctrines affirmed by many conservative evangelicals within the traditional church. He holds to a complementarian understanding of gender roles, the inspiration and inerrancy of the Scripture, and the propitiatory death of Christ.[12] However, his desire to engage nonbelievers missionally has led him to adopt the slogan "theologically conservative and culturally liberal" to describe his ministry.[13]

While the idea of Christian beer brewers and rock band managers might make some socially conservative Christians uncomfortable, for Driscoll such things simply arise from a healthy desire to emulate Jesus' missionary lifestyle. In his published works, he spends a rather lengthy amount of time attacking so-called Christian legalists who, in his mind, erect unnecessary dividing walls between the church and the lost. For example, in one autobiographical section he writes, "I learned that God's mission is not to create a team of moral and decent people but rather to create a movement of holy loving missionaries who are comfortable and truthful around lost sinners and who, in this way, look more like Jesus than most of his pastors do."[14]

Driscoll's book.

11. Ibid., 40.

12. For a survey of Driscoll's theology consider, Mark Driscoll, "Emerging Church and Biblicist Theology," 21–47. See also Driscoll and Breshears, *Doctrine*.

13. Driscoll, *Confessions of a Reformission Rev.*, 46. This phrase also appears in Driscoll, *Radical Reformission*, 22.

14. Driscoll, *Confessions of a Reformission Rev.*, 35.

Baptists and the Emerging Church Movement

Mark Driscoll on Contextualization

Driscoll's reformissional proposal does not simply end with a call to engage nonbelievers outside of the church. He also argues that churches must contextualize their ministries to fit their surrounding culture if they wish to minister effectively. He insists Christians should first "be particularly attentive to both the culture they live in and the other cultures they encounter."[15] After believers gain knowledge of their culture, they should then carefully begin the contextualization process. Citing Paul's statements in 1 Corinthians 9:19–23 as biblical warrant, Driscoll writes that "reformission churches have to continually examine and adjust their musical styles, websites, aesthetics, acoustics, programming, and just about everything but their Bible in an effort to effectively communicate the Gospel to as many people as possible in the cultures around them."[16]

Because Driscoll ministers in Seattle, Washington, his church has, in the name of contextualization, absorbed some of the cultural ethos of this rather unique American city. After his church sings with a worship band that plays "moody chords evocative of indie rock,"[17] Driscoll takes the platform to preach. He wears what some have described as the "hip pastor uniform," typically jeans and an untucked shirt.[18] The *Seattle Times* reports that Driscoll

> is deeply in touch with the culture of his congregants: the hard-edged, high-tech, disaffected sensibility of the bands they love (Modest Mouse, Death Cab for Cutie), the films they watch ("The Matrix," "Fight Club"), and

---

15. Driscoll, *Radical Reformission*, 93. Elsewhere Driscoll instructs his readers to become careful observers of their culture by doing such things as watching local television, listening to talk radio, watching people in the grocery store, and observing the types of magazines people purchase. Driscoll, *Vintage Church*, 224–27.

16. Driscoll, *Radical Reformission*, 100.

17. Ibid.

18. Hansen, "Pastor Provocateur," 44.

Assessing Emerging Church Missional Ministry

the art they appreciate (no gauzy Jesus-on-the-beach paintings, please). He loves that culture himself.[19]

Clearly, Driscoll's church "fits" the culture of Seattle rather well.

Of all of his efforts at contextualization, however, perhaps Driscoll's preaching style has garnered the most attention. Though Driscoll boldly and unapologetically proclaims gospel truth, he does so in a manner that some find to be edgy.[20] John Bohannon has labeled Driscoll's style "Seattle Street Preaching" because of his use of language commonly found on the streets of Seattle.[21] Indeed, Driscoll does sometimes employ rather crass humor to make his point, frequently using sexual innuendoes and, in his words, making "fun of every conceivable group of people."[22]

Driscoll's personality and background obviously play a role in shaping his preaching style. However, Driscoll does make it clear that many times he deliberately chooses his blunt language in the pulpit to communicate with his Seattle listeners. He believes that reaching Seattle with the gospel "demands new, creative ways"[23] of ministry and understands his blunt style of preaching to fall in this category. For example, concerning his occasional use of crude humor in the pulpit, he writes, "Humor is a missiological ministry tool that is necessary for successful evangelism in our culture."[24] Bohannon, commenting upon Driscoll's preaching style, explains,

---

19. Tu, "Pastor Mark Packs 'Em In."

20. Critics of Driscoll, and his style of preaching, are almost too numerous to mention. However, for an overview, consider Kelly, "Driscoll's Vulgarity Draws Media Attention." Driscoll is perhaps most famous for being the "cussing pastor," a label ascribed to him by Donald Miller in Miller, *Blue Like Jazz*, 134. However, since the publication of Miller's book, Driscoll has expressed regret over his use of profanity in the pulpit. See, for example, Stetzer, "Interview with Mark Driscoll."

21. Bohannon, "Preaching and the Emerging Church Movement," 319.

22. Driscoll, *Religion Saves*, 45. Also consider Driscoll's explanation of his preaching methodology in Driscoll, "How Sharp the Edge?" For a description of the kind of blunt preaching that Driscoll often practices, see Worthen, "Who Would Jesus Smack Down?"

23. Hansen, *Young, Restless, and Reformed*, 146.

24. Driscoll, *Religion Saves*, 64.

"Driscoll sees himself as a missionary to Seattle . . . he therefore has no trouble wearing the same clothes, *speaking the same words*, and listening to the same music—all for the sake of the Gospel."[25]

Assessing Driscoll on Missional Living and the Contextualization Process

Before I consider Driscoll's use of the multisite church model— the third and final component of Driscoll's means of missional engagement—I will pause to assess the two proposals surveyed thus far. Three major points of discussion are appropriate in light of Driscoll's arguments.

First, Christians of all backgrounds can and should endorse Driscoll's call for church members to view themselves as missionaries engaging a non-Christian world. Attractional evangelism, an evangelism method that relies upon attracting people to a church building, can no longer be the primary evangelistic strategy for the church in a post-Christian world.[26] Working in an extremely secular context, Driscoll rightly emphasizes a missional lifestyle that calls members to engage nonbelievers with the gospel where they live.

Certainly, some people may take issue with the *way* in which Driscoll carries out his missional engagement. One thinks, for example, of the controversies caused by Driscoll's stories of beer brewers and tattoo artists. However, before criticizing Driscoll too strongly, such people must remember the cultural context in which Driscoll lives. In a city devoid of much Christian influence, the only way to engage many young people is to meet them in places not typically associated with Christianity. This is not to say

---

25. Bohannon, *Preaching and the Emerging Church*, 326, emphasis added.

26. Driscoll details the attractional method and why it alone is not sufficient in our post-Christian culture in Driscoll, *Reformission*, 65–83. Other writers not associated with the emerging movement have made similar comments regarding the failure of attractional method. See, for example, Stetzer and Putman, *Breaking the Missional Code*, 44–72; Slaughter, *Change the World*, 1–10.

Assessing Emerging Church Missional Ministry

that one must condone or participate in all of the sinful behaviors present in a non-Christian culture (more on that in a moment).[27] However, one can, as Driscoll suggests, follow in the footsteps of a missionary savior who fellowshipped with sinners and explained theology to social outcasts.[28]

Second, one can praise Driscoll for retaining his firm theological and ethical convictions while engaging in his missional and contextualization work. Contrary to popular opinion, Driscoll does not advocate a complete capitulation to modern culture. He warns:

> Because the postmodern fascination with the present leads to the same sort of cultural worldliness as is rebuked in Paul's letters to the Corinthians, we must contend that there is an eternal state marked by God's kingdom that takes preeminence over any culture and its faddish trends in defining faithful Christianity.[29]

Driscoll's convictional thinking here reflects the kind of thought that much of the emerging movement both needs and lacks. In his most extensive work on missional engagement, Driscoll even provides his readers with a chart entitled "Biblical Principles for Cultural Decision Making."[30] There, Driscoll offers Scripture passages to help aspiring missional Christians know what parts of a culture to reject and what parts of a culture to accept. He outlines guiding questions like, "Would this be beneficial to me personally and the Gospel generally . . . will I be doing this activity in the

---

27. For example, though Driscoll famously speaks of alcohol and Christian beer brewers, he bluntly condemns drunkenness. In a chapter explaining his view on alcohol he writes, "All Bible believing Christians agree that drunkenness is a sin that causes a life of misery. In addition, Christians are to obey their government in regard to alcohol consumption, which means that such things as underage drinking in America are sinful (Rom. 13:1–7)." Driscoll, *Radical Reformission*, 148.

28. While many biblical examples are available, perhaps Jesus' frequent meals with sinful people are the most important to consider. For an extensive examination of these, consider Blomberg, *Contagious Holiness*.

29. Driscoll, "Church and the Supremacy of Christ," 139.

30. See Driscoll, *Radical Reformission*, 104.

presence of someone who I know will fall into sin as a result . . . and can I do this with a clear conscience?"[31]

Third, one can legitimately criticize Driscoll for occasionally failing to live up to the very convictions that he espouses. Though he speaks of the need to have "Biblical principles for cultural decision making," perhaps his ministry would be more profitable, and certainly less controversial, if he more carefully applied such principles to himself. For example, commenting upon Driscoll's preaching style, John MacArthur has written, "It would certainly be accurate to describe both his vocabulary and his subject matter at times as tasteless, indecent, crude, and utterly inappropriate for a minister of Christ. In every message I listened to, at least once he veered into territory that ought to be clearly marked off limits for the pulpit."[32] John Piper has expressed similar concerns, albeit in a more modest fashion.[33]

These respected pastors indeed have a point. One wonders how employing jokes about sex acts during a sermon can, in Driscoll's words, "benefit me personally and the Gospel generally."[34] Certainly, given his context, Driscoll must address sexual matters with bluntness and candor. Yet, no sufficient reason exists for him to employ crudeness.[35] Though Driscoll speaks well about carefully assessing our post-Christian culture through the lens of the gospel, crude and irreverent joking should certainly be the part of the culture that we reject, not accept.[36]

---

31. Ibid.

32. MacArthur, "Grunge Christianity?," n.p.

33. Piper spoke of this at the 2006 Desiring God Conference. Joshua Harris offers an accurate summation of Piper's words at Josh Harris, "Desiring God 2006: Day Two."

34. This is the first question in Driscoll's "Biblical Principles for Cultural Engagement."

35. A perfect example would be the recent discussion surrounding Driscoll's book on marriage, *Real Marriage*. Certainly the book has much to commend it. However, it has sparked controversy partly because of Driscoll's rather unnecessary use of graphic language. For a fair assessment, consider Challies, review of *Real Marriage*.

36. Consider Eph 5:4.

Mark Driscoll on the Multisite Church

Introduction to the Mars Hill Multisite Model

The desire for a missional lifestyle has also led Driscoll to enthusiastically support the multisite church model, the third aspect of his program for missional engagement. Driscoll insists that missional churches should employ "modern technology such as blogging and video" in an effort to become a "missionary in [the] local culture."[37] He believes that the multisite church model and its attendant use of new technology offer a way for churches to become fruitful missionaries who make use of today's digital tools. He has therefore adopted the multisite church model as a key component of his missional strategy, and he addresses this topic extensively in his most complete work on ecclesiology, *Vintage Church*.[38]

Driscoll claims that his church embraced the multisite model long before it developed popularity within certain segments of evangelicalism. Soon after his church's inception, his church had the opportunity to use multiple meeting sites, and Driscoll seized this opportunity out of a desire to reach as many people as possible.[39] As his church has expanded, it has continued to make use

---

37. Driscoll, *Religion Saves*, 212. Elsewhere Driscoll defends his use of the multisite model as a means to reach more people by writing, "Paul says, we must use 'all means' to win as many people to Jesus as possible. If multiple campuses and video are ways that God the Holy Spirit chooses to reach more people for Jesus, then we would be wise to not criticize or oppose it, even if our church decides not to do it." Driscoll and Breshears, *Vintage Church*, 259.

38. Certainly, churches do not have to be connected to the emerging church or missional church movements to employ the multisite strategy. Recently, a large number of evangelical congregations not associated with these movements have begun to embrace multisite ministry. The author here is only pointing out that Driscoll understands the multisite model to be a key component of what it means for *his* church to be missional. Therefore, though there are a number of multisite church models, in this chapter the author will only consider the model employed by Driscoll's church as it directly relates to the purposes of this work. For a description of different multisite models, see Surratt et al., *Multi-Site Church Revolution*, 26–42.

39. Driscoll tells this story in Driscoll, *Vintage Church*, 243–56.

of the multisite model. At the time of this writing, his church now encompasses eleven different locations in different states.[40]

Originally, Driscoll's church, Mars Hill Church, considered all of its locations as campuses of one large church. However, his church has recently relabeled these individual locations as churches. These eleven different churches have their own pastoral team, worship leaders, and membership lists. However, readers should not construe this to mean that eleven completely autonomous churches exist within the Mars Hill Network. The Mars Hill website states, "Though by definition we may be many different churches, the Mars Hill Network of churches remains a single, united church. We share a common infrastructure, a common mission, common teaching, and a common belief that we can reach more people by working together rather than existing separately."[41]

The multisite church model has generated much discussion lately, though unfortunately few substantive theological critiques have appeared.[42] However, Baptists should have an interest in the theological implications of new ecclesiological proposals. Baptists, therefore, should not shrink from a careful theological assessment of the multisite model, especially when employed on such a large scale as Driscoll's church. While one could certainly discuss many aspects of Driscoll's multisite model, here I will concentrate only on two facets of the Mars Hill Network. First, I will consider the relational implications of having one church that meets in eleven

---

40. This is the current make-up of Mars Hill Network. See Mars Hill Church Website, "Locations and Services," http://marshill.com/locations_and_services.

41. Originally at Mars Hill website, "No More Mars Hill 'Campuses,'" http://marshill.com/2011/08/08/no-more-mars-hill-campuses; see Murashko, "Mars Hill Church: Don't Call Us 'Campuses' Anymore," http://www.christianpost.com/news/mars-hill-church-dont-call-us-campuses-anymore-53736.

42. Many works dedicated to the multisite movement have recently appeared. Yet, few give much attention to theological concerns. Instead, they concentrate primarily on offering practical advice. Consider Surratt et al., *Multi-Site Church Revolution*; McConnell, *Multi-Site Churches*; Surratt et al., *Multi-Site Road Trip*. However, one noteworthy work that does offer some theological assessment of the multisite movement is Frye, "Multi-Site Church Phenomenon in North America: 1950–2010."

Assessing Emerging Church Missional Ministry

different locations and spans differing states. Second, I will offer a theological critique from historic Baptist convictions related to the fact that the Mars Hill model considers eleven different "churches" to constitute one unified church.

Relational Implications

The New Testament clearly calls for unity within the Christian church. Paul, for example, teaches about the unity of the body in 1 Corinthians 12:12, and he commands unity in Ephesians 4:3-5. Throughout church history, many theologians have focused their discussions regarding church unity on what it means for the church universal to display unity.[43] While this discussion is important, one should note that most New Testament epistles were written to local churches. This focus on the local church reveals that God intends Christian unity to be expressed in the local church as well.

Unity finds expression in several different aspects of local church life. Scripture identifies shared theological convictions as an important and necessary component of a unified church. Paul, for example, spoke of a shared faith, i.e., "one faith" in Ephesians 4:1-6. In addition, when speaking of unity, some theologians have highlighted the sense of unity that comes from a shared ministry philosophy or organizational plan.[44]

However, John Hammett reminds us that, "Most often, the oneness of a local congregation in the New Testament seems to be relational, rooted in the relationships among the members."[45]

---

43. Irenaeus emphasized doctrinal agreement as a key component of unity. Irenaeus, *Against Heresies*, bk. 1, 10, 2. Cyprian grounded unity in communion with the church's bishops in *On the Unity of the Catholic Church*. The Protestant reformers emphasized unity as a more spiritual concept—unity around the gospel. Avis, *Church in the Theology of the Reformers*, 2-4.

44. See Driscoll and Breshears, *Vintage Church*, 137-40. Driscoll and Breshears mention unity around such things as a common ministry philosophy. However, they also emphasize the importance of shared theological commitments.

45. Hammett, "What Makes a Multi-Site Church One Church?," 6. Hammett offers several texts to support his point, highlighting passages that

Hammett's statement is a good reminder that, though church unity is not less than a shared commitment to theology, it does involve more than that. The New Testament's descriptions of church life envision deep relational commitments within the church. God desires that believers relate to one another intimately within the church and that they model the gospel by displaying unity in these relationships.

This fact immediately raises questions about how the original Mars Hill Church model, which consisted of eleven campuses constituting one large church, could adequately display the sort of relational unity depicted in the New Testament. In the original Mars Hill model, a shared theology and "a common infrastructure, a common mission, and a common teaching"[46] unified the campuses. Nevertheless, members of the Mars Hill campus in Arizona could have no relational unity with the members of Mars Hill campus in Seattle. Distance would have prevented them, for example, from sharing the Lord's Supper as a unified body (1 Cor 10:16–17) or from exercising informed, corporate church discipline together (1 Cor 5:4–5). Perhaps this consideration, at least in part, promoted Mars Hill Church to recently re-label its individual sites churches instead of campuses. Mars Hill Church should receive praise for this move because this transition alleviates some concerns related to relational unity.

However, a key concern does remain. The new Mars Hill model does not sufficiently address the relationship between the church's leadership and its members. The New Testament speaks of this relationship rather frequently in its descriptions of relational unity. For example, the New Testament instructs the members of a local church to promote relational unity by following pastoral leadership (e.g., 1 Thess 5:12–13). It also tells local church members to hold a church's pastoral leadership accountable for such

---

describe the church fellowshipping together (Acts 2:44; 4:32), passages that speak of the unity of the body of Christ (Rom 12; 1 Cor 12), and passages that offer instructions related to maintaining unity in relationships (1 Cor 1:10; Phil 2:2).

46. Originally at Mars Hill website, "No More Mars Hill 'Campuses'"; see Murashko, "Mars Hill Church: Don't Call Us 'Campuses' Anymore."

things as moral or doctrinal failures (1 Tim 5:17–19) in order to preserve the witness of the church.

To their credit, Driscoll and the leaders of Mars Hill Church understand the need for pastoral leadership and accountability within each local church body, and they call for campus pastors to serve at each Mars Hill location.[47] Campus pastors in the Mars Hill model are able to make leadership decisions related to their local church body and can occasionally preach to their congregations. However, the primary responsibility for preaching and leading still belongs to Mark Driscoll. Around 80 percent of the time, church attenders at the various Mars Hill churches will view Driscoll's sermons via a digital broadcast.[48]

Herein lies the problem. If the Mars Hill sites exist as individual churches, then one must ask why Driscoll, someone who exists outside of each local congregation, does the vast majority of each church's preaching. Driscoll does most of the preaching in each Mars Hill church, but he is technically only a member of the main church in Seattle.[49] Can attenders at the Mars Hill location in California hold Driscoll responsible for the content of his preaching when they receive it digitally from Seattle? Would they be able to discipline Driscoll for false teaching or would such a responsibility reside with the elder board of the Seattle church? Such things are certainly part of the relationship envisioned between a local church and its pastor in 1 Timothy 5:17–19, and they are critical for the kind of relational unity the New Testament envisions

---

47. Discussions related to campus pastors and local church leadership can be found in Driscoll and Breshears, *Vintage Church*, 253–54.

48. Ibid. Driscoll states that campus pastors fill the pulpit around ten to twelve times per year when the primary preacher in the network, i.e., himself, is unavailable.

49. Driscoll argues that a person's church membership must be connected to the local Mars Hill Church site that person attends, not with the Mars Hill Network *in toto*. See Driscoll and Breshears, *Vintage Church*, 254–55. This fact means that the preacher most Mars Hill attenders regularly hear (Driscoll) is not a member of their church, complicating opportunities for relational accountability.

for the local church.⁵⁰ These unanswered questions accentuate the relational and accountability issues that are left unresolved in the new Mars Hill model.

Theological Implications

Some of the difficulty here no doubt stems from the fact that the new Mars Hill model itself is not sufficiently clear. Though the organization describes its multiple locations as individual churches, it also states, "The Mars Hill Network of churches remains a single, united church."⁵¹ At first, this language appears somewhat contradictory, particularly to Baptist readers, as it is difficult to discern how a network of individual churches can still constitute one church.⁵² Whatever the Mars Hill Network intends by this wording, individual congregations do lack complete autonomy in this model. Each local site shares the same primary preaching pastor, Mark Driscoll, and each site deeply connects itself to the Mars Hill leadership structure based in Seattle.

One begins to wonder, then, what sort of church model from history adequately describes the Mars Hill Network. Some will no doubt argue that the Mars Hill model represents some sort of Episcopalian church structure, for they will perceive Driscoll, in his capacity as lead teacher and vision caster, to be acting as a sort of bishop over the Mars Hill locations.⁵³ Though Driscoll does have considerable influence in this model, it is not

---

50. In addition, Baptists will certainly argue that the congregation should retain the right to hire and fire pastoral leadership, because this is a component of congregational polity. However, could a local Mars Hill site successful fire Driscoll, as he is not a member of their local body?

51. Originally at Mars Hill website, "No More Mars Hill 'Campuses'"; see Murashko, "Mars Hill Church: Don't Call Us 'Campuses' Anymore."

52. This statement would perhaps cause less trouble for readers with a background in a church with a more connectional ecclesiology.

53. Some critics have levied this criticism against the multisite approach in general. It seems they would certainly view the Mars Hill model in a similar fashion. Consider White and Yeats, *Franchising McChurch*, 81–82, 154–56, 191.

Assessing Emerging Church Missional Ministry

to the extent of an authoritative bishop.[54] Therefore, this criticism is not completely apt.

Other thinkers, while not necessarily arguing that Driscoll has become akin to a bishop, will likely contend that the Mars Hill model still represents some form of connectionalism. Grant Gaines, for example, believes that

> because multiple sites equal multiple churches, there is actually no such thing as a multi-site church. There are simply multi-*church* groups or associations that are connected under one governing structure and that have chosen to call themselves a multi-site church. In this way, multi-site church structure is nothing new. It is simply connectionalism, and it has been around for generations.[55]

Gaines offers this critique of all multisite models, and he would doubtlessly critique Driscoll's church along these lines. The Mars Hill model does explicitly claim that individual churches exist and that they are united in such a way that one should consider them as part of a single, unified church. However, the governing structure that unites the individual Mars Hill churches is rather loose and it is not as developed as the sort typically found in denominations that hold to a connectionalist understanding of ecclesiology. Therefore, the Mars Hill model does not sufficiently represent a model of connectionalism either.

This author views the Mars Hill model as a new ecclesiological development with no clear historic parallels.[56] Digital

---

54. Brian Frye does an excellent job detailing why it is incorrect to claim that multisite churches by necessity lead to something akin to an Episcopalian church structure. His comments certainly apply to this potential critique of the Mars Hill model. See Frye, "Multi-Site Church Phenomenon," 200–204. Driscoll himself answers this charge in Driscoll and Breshears, *Vintage Church*, 265–66.

55. Gaines argues that a true multisite church cannot technically exist because, according to his thinking, the New Testament exegetically requires Christians to consider individual campuses as churches. Gaines, "Exegetical Critique of Multi-Site."

56. One must remember that, contrary to most multisite proponents, the

technology, along with a highly mobile society, has afforded the opportunity for such a model to exist. However, regardless of its historic significance, Baptists should have some concern over this new model. Historically, Baptists have strongly advocated for the autonomy of a local church congregation. Though early Baptists valued cooperation among congregations, and hence formed associations, they considered each church as bearing the ultimate responsibility for its own behavior.[57] In contrast, the Mars Hill model considers individual churches to exist as one unified church with a shared preaching pastor. A church would seemingly have a difficult time claiming autonomy when it has relegated its teaching and preaching to someone outside of its own membership. Also, because Mars Hill churches exist as part of one larger church, clearly their obligations to one another will be greater than if they were autonomous yet cooperating churches as is typical in much of Baptist life.[58]

In time, as the Mars Hill Network continues to mature, it may well assuage this author's concerns. After all, one must remember the relative youth of the network. When its leaders relabeled their individual sites as churches, rather than campuses of one large church, they displayed wisdom and a desire for biblical faithfulness. Their commitment to Scripture and their willingness to adapt offers hope that they will continue to perfect their model as it matures and expands.

Mars Hill model does not claim to be one church meeting in multiple campuses. Rather, it claims to be multiple churches unified as one church.

57. On cooperation between Baptist churches see Wamble, "Concept and Practice."

58. The fact that Mars Hill Church recently adopted several executive elders to oversee the entire Mars Hill network compounds this problem. These executive elders apparently exercise direction over all of the churches in the Mars Hill Church network. See "Leadership at Mars Hill Church," http://marshill.com/leadership.

Revisionists and the Meaning of Missional

Revisionists typically employ the term missional in a different manner from Driscoll. Revisionists use the term to describe their desire for the church to become involved in all manner of social and political causes. They speak of the need for church participation in environmental, political, cultural, and social issues and hope that such work will help to usher in God's kingdom way of living upon this earth. In this section, I will first give attention to these writers' understanding of the church's mission and then to its attendant emphasis on the kingdom of God. Because Brian McLaren has prolifically written on this subject, I will give special attention to his works, though other revisionist leaders will also receive attention.

The Revisionist Understanding of the Mission of the Church

Revisionist leaders believe that the traditional church has truncated the mission of the church by focusing upon spiritual concerns to the neglect of physical needs. Brian McLaren writes of the emotions he felt while he was part of a traditional church:

> Over the years a feeling grew within me, usually vague but sometimes acute, that I was missing something, perhaps something important. Jesus' cross in the past saved me from hell in the future, but it was hard to be clear on what it meant for me in the struggle in the present. And more importantly, did the Gospel have anything to say about justice for the many, not just the justification of the individual? Was the Gospel intended to give hope for human cultures and the created order of history?[59]

---

59. McLaren, *Generous Orthodoxy*, 55. Elsewhere McLaren writes that the traditional church's emphasis upon personal salvation has turned the gospel into "an individualistic theory, an abstraction with personal but not global import." See McLaren, *Generous Orthodoxy*, 24.

Baptists and the Emerging Church Movement

In McLaren's mind, the traditional church, much like the religious leaders of Jesus' day, has confused and distorted the real message of Scripture. He answers this perceived distortion by speaking of a *secret* message of Jesus, a message that the traditional church has lost but that emerging Christians must now work to recover. He writes, "I've become convinced that [Jesus' message] has everything to do with public matters in general and politics in particular—including economics and aid, personal empowerment and choice, foreign policy and war."[60]

In his published works, McLaren calls on the emerging church to concern itself with a variety of social and political issues in order to faithfully represent this supposed real message of Jesus. He writes:

> Yes, I believe that the Gospel has facts that deal with forgiveness of sins, but I feel unfaithful to Jesus to define the Gospel by that one facet when I see our contemporary churches failing to address so many other essential Gospel concerns- justice, compassion, sacrifice, purpose, transformation into Christlikeness, and ultimate hope.[61]

Environmental regulation, economic inequality, global politics, and issues of war and peace are matters that receive particular attention from McLaren.[62]

Other revisionist leaders echo McLaren's sentiments. Gibbs and Bolger, after conducting extensive research on the emerging church movement, concluded, "Social service is integral to the [emerging] church's understanding of discipleship. Members of emerging churches do not separate the Great Commission . . . from the Great Commandment."[63] They quote one member of the emerging movement, Kenny Mitchell, as saying, "as a church, we

---

60. McLaren, *Secret Message of Jesus*, 10.

61. McLaren, "Method, Message," 213.

62. His most extensive treatment of these issues can be found in McLaren, *Everything Must Change*.

63. Gibbs and Bolger, *Emerging Churches*, 149.

must be socially and politically aware . . . we have to be engaged in what Jesus talked about."[64]

Assessing the Revisionist Understanding of Mission

This call for broader missional engagement deserves a careful assessment. In this section, I will offer three brief remarks related the revisionist understanding of the church's mission. In the subsequent section, I will survey and assess how revisionists view the kingdom of God, making use of the work of several prominent Baptist theologians.

First, while one can praise revisionist leaders for their concern for poverty and social justice, their inaccurate caricatures of most Christians within the so-called traditional church invite serious questions. As noted, leaders such as McLaren condemn the traditional church for a supposed lack of interest in social needs. However, history offers numerous examples of rather "traditional church" Christians who personally excelled at both proclaiming the gospel and performing social work. Many historians credit Christianity with a number of positive developments in Western civilization, including such things as hospitals, women's rights, education, and the abolition of slavery.[65] Revisionist leaders therefore simply err when they claim that so-called traditional church Christians have failed to engage social needs because of a preoccupation with preaching the gospel. Perhaps some of these leaders at one time personally experienced a Christian tradition devoid of any kind of social work. Brian McLaren certainly alludes to this in some of his writings. While this is unfortunate, it is not sufficient reason for these leaders to incorrectly caricature everyone in the traditional church.

Second, though revisionist leaders criticize traditional churches for not participating in activities associated with their

---

64. Ibid., 142. This is the testimony of Kenny Mitchell, as recorded by Gibbs and Bolger.

65. See, for example, Schmidt, *How Christianity Changed the World*; Hill, *What Has Christianity Ever Done for Us?*

enlarged understanding of missional ministry, it is not clear from the New Testament that such activities are part of the local church's prescribed mission. Kevin DeYoung and Greg Gilbert explain that the mission of the church "is not everything we do in Jesus' name, nor everything we do in obedience to Christ. Mission is the task we are given to fulfill."[66] They argue that we should consider Christ's statements in Matthew 28:16–20, Mark 13:10, Luke 24:44–49, and Acts 1:8 to be Christ's mission for the church. In light of these texts, they conclude that the church's mission is primarily to "win people to Christ and build them up in Christ."[67]

Despite the moral goodness of social work, political involvement, and environmental cleanup, DeYoung and Gilbert are correct when they note that neither Christ nor Paul portrayed such activities as the church's mission.[68] This fact suggests that such activities should not receive the weight they do in some revisionist

---

66. DeYoung and Gilbert, *What Is the Mission*, 29. Certainly many evangelicals will disagree with this claim and argue that the entire Bible details the mission of God and, by consequence, the mission of God's people. While the Bible testifies to the mission of God, it seems best, in my judgment, to not assume that the mission of God as found in all the Bible is *necessarily* the mission that is given to God's people. In taking this approach, I obviously do not speak for all Baptists, because many Baptists have offered favorable reviews of the work of such theologians as Christopher Wright. DeYoung and Gilbert take an approach similar to mine and argue, "Isn't it better to locate our responsibility in the tasks we are given rather than in the work we see God accomplishing?" Ibid., 42. Cf. Wright, *Mission of God*. For a charitable critique of Wright's approach, consider Millar, "Biblical Theology of Mission."

67. DeYoung and Gilbert, *What Is the Mission*, 40–44.

68. I am not suggesting that individual Christians should not participate in such activities—they should—or that it is somehow sinful for churches to involve themselves in such projects. I am merely arguing that such activities are not necessarily the church's prescribed mission. On this point, consider Mouw, "Carl Henry Was Right." Mouw draws from Kuyper's distinction between the gathered church and individual Christians to explain that, while individual Christians can and should involve themselves in political, economic, and social work, the church should retain a singular focus on the gospel of Christ. See also Horton, *Gospel Commission*, 210–46. Cf. Wright, *Mission of God's People*; Stott, *Christian Mission in the Modern World*, 25–28. For work on Paul's understanding of the church's mission, see Plummer, *Paul's Understanding of the Church's Mission*.

Assessing Emerging Church Missional Ministry

literature, at least in regards to the mission of a local church. In short, Christ gave his church a specific mission to fulfill, and no one person should supplement it, much less replace it, with desires of his or her own.

Third, while revisionist leaders place a strong emphasis upon social and political work they many times neglect, or even deny, the gospel message. As noted, revisionist calls for broad missional engagement "flatten" the mission of the church to the point that any morally good act can be considered part of the church's mission. In such a construct, the proclamation of the gospel becomes just one project among many. It becomes far too easy for one to neglect the gospel or even deny the gospel out of a desire for fruitful and culturally acceptable social work in the here and now.

It appears that such a thing has unfortunately occurred among many in the revisionist stream of the emerging church movement. One revisionist writer describes service in God's kingdom as opposition to nationalism and social injustice, but makes no mention of proclaiming peace with God through Christ.[69] Others speak of merely living a lifestyle of service to others without sharing a gospel witness. They believe "their daily lives point to the reality of the kingdom" and that "through their daily activities in the community, members preach the good news."[70]

McLaren represents a particularly egregious example of this trend. He rejects central tenets of the gospel in order to reformulate the Christian message into a call for social and political involvement.[71] In *The Secret Message of Jesus*, for example, he never explains the gospel, a troubling fact considering that he claims the book reveals Jesus's central message. Instead, he interprets gospel texts such as John 3 ("must be born again") and Paul's statements regarding reconciliation between God and man as descriptors of

---

69. See Canosa, "I Pledge Allegiance to the Kingdom," 141–49.

70. Gibbs and Bolger, *Emerging Churches*, 59.

71. Many have noted McLaren's objections to the penal substitution model of the atonement as well as his aversion to other important Christian doctrines. See, for example, Craigen, "Emergent Soteriology," 177–90; Carson, *Becoming Conversant*, 157–82.

social change on this earth.⁷² Michael Horton warns that at this point, Christians have two options, "The first is to say, with McLaren, that the Gospel is a call to love God and our neighbors—and this is salvation. The second is to say, with the Scriptures . . . that the Gospel consists exclusively in the announcement of what God has done to redeem his creation in Christ."⁷³

In the end, the revisionist calls for social and political activism, with no accompanying focus on Christ's gospel, transform Christianity into just another moral law that one must obey. The unbalanced focus on social work actually flips the gospel on its head, making the central message of Christianity about the works people do for God rather than trusting in the work God has done for people through Christ. Though Baptists can praise emerging writers for their desire for helpful social and political engagement, they should not follow them into a mission that minimizes or confuses the gospel.

Revisionists on Kingdom of God and Mission

Emerging Christians believe a focus upon the kingdom of God should be the interpretive lens one uses to understand all of God's work.⁷⁴ An emphasis on the kingdom of God is certainly at the center of their call for a broader understanding of the church's mission. McLaren writes that we must "see, seek, receive, and enter a new political and social and spiritual reality that [Jesus] calls the kingdom (or empire) of God, or the kingdom (or empire) of heaven."⁷⁵ This statement reveals why McLaren's strongly connects his calls for social engagement with his discussions of God's kingdom. For McLaren, the kingdom of God primarily entails a

---

72. McLaren, *Secret Message of Jesus*, 37, 100–101.

73. Horton, *Gospel Commission*, 245.

74. Miles explains, "Many emerging church leaders have chosen to utilize the Kingdom of God as the paradigm for their previsioning of church theology and praxis." Miles, "Kingdom without a King?," 88.

75. McLaren, *Secret Message of Jesus*, 17.

new "social and spiritual" reality here on this earth.[76] In his line of thinking, when one rebels against the unjust arrangements of this fallen world by practicing the message of Jesus, they are actually participating in ushering in the kingdom of God. McLaren essentially sees his pleas for social engagement as calls for an ushering in of God's kingdom ideal upon this earth. Other emerging leaders speak in a manner similar to McLaren. Ray Anderson, an influential theologian for emerging Christians, writes that followers of Christ "participate in the messianic mission to extend the kingdom into every crevice and corner of the world."[77]

Assessing Revisionist Understanding of Kingdom of God

With statements such as these, one can see that revisionist proponents are quite ambitious. They boldly call for the church to work to expand the kingdom of God on this earth by creating the social conditions they associate with God's kingly rule. Revisionists are right to call attention to the kingdom of God because the New Testament, particularly the gospels, refers to the kingdom quite often. However, there are deficiencies in their understanding of the kingdom, and it is important to consider them as they have bearing on the emerging church's understanding of mission. Here I will offer two critiques, making use of the work of prominent Baptist theologians such as Ladd, Dargan, and Moore.

First, some revisionist leaders appear to pit the kingdom of God against the church in an unhealthy manner. Ray Anderson

---

76. For example, in his most extensive treatment on the subject, McLaren reduces the kingdom of God down to: (1) an emphasis upon the poor and outcasts, (2) inward sincerity of the heart, (3) judgment on injustice and hypocrisy, and (4) a possible new order for our present world. McLaren, *Secret Message of Jesus*, 22–23.

77. Anderson, *Emergent Theology*, 115. In addition, Gibbs and Bolger note that many emerging churches believe "the kingdom, or the reign of God, is about our life here and now" and write "the Gospel of emerging churches is not confined to personal salvation [but] is the social transformation arising from the presence and permeation of the reign of Christ." Gibbs and Bolger, *Emerging Churches*, 63.

informs his readers, "The Spirit of Christ calls us to be disciples of the kingdom rather than the church."[78] Dieter Zander even goes so far as to argue that a focus on the kingdom has freed him from the Christian church. He states, "I needed a fast from the system [the church and its perceived bureaucracy]. It is not about the church but about the kingdom. The kingdom transcends all forms."[79] For these and other emerging leaders, the church has become an optional appendage to the Christian life while "real" Christian service consists in advancing God's kingdom outside of the church. For this reason, Gibbs and Bolger note that emerging Christians typically "do not seek to start churches *per se* but to foster communities that embody the kingdom. Whether a community explicitly becomes a church is not the immediate goal. The priority is that the kingdom is expressed."[80]

Emerging leaders are correct when they note that church and kingdom of God are not completely synonymous. However, they do miss the important relationship that exists between the two entities. The Baptist theologian George Eldon Ladd described that relationship in this way: "The kingdom creates the church, works through the church, and is proclaimed in the world by the church. There can be no kingdom without a church—those who have acknowledged God's rule—and there can be no church without God's kingdom."[81] In short, the church has immense significance because it has been entrusted with the message of the kingdom, the gospel, and it has been called to represent the kingdom lifestyle in a fallen world.

Baptists have certainly spoken of this close relationship between church and kingdom throughout their history. The First London Confession states, "Christ hath here on earth a spitituall Kingdome, which is the Church, which he hath purchased and

---

78. Anderson, *Emergent Theology*, 111.

79. Gibbs and Bolger, *Emerging Churches*, 60. This is the testimony of Dieter Zander as recorded by Gibbs and Bolger.

80. Ibid., 61.

81. Ladd, *Theology of the New Testament*, 117.

Assessing Emerging Church Missional Ministry

redeemed to himselfe as a peculiar inheritance."[82] When they wrote this statement, the early Baptists were arguing against the Church of England's wedding of civil and ecclesiastical power. With this wording, they attempted to highlight the fact that the church, not temporal political institutions, displays Christ's kingdom.[83] Russell Moore, a contemporary Baptist writer, represents this line of thinking well when he writes, "Righteousness and justice of the messianic order cannot be found, in the present age, in the arenas of political, social, economic, or academic orders. Instead, the reign of Christ is focused in this age solely on His reign as Messiah over the people called into the kingdom, namely, those who make up his church."[84]

Therefore, rather than attempting to bring about kingdom change in contemporary political, economic, or social organizations, it seems revisionist Christians would do well to focus primarily on Christ's church. They should expend their energies on creating churches that reveal the gospel, not trying to mold secular institutions to fit the values of Christ's kingdom. As Baptist theologian E. C. Dargan has written, "The relations of church and kingdom are necessarily close. The effective instrument for carrying on the kingdom in this world is the church."[85]

Second, revisionists fail to understand what constitutes true kingdom work. As previously noted, they describe their ministry philosophy as a partnering with God to expand his kingdom and its influence on this earth. This language is troublesome because the New Testament portrays God's people as receiving entrance into the kingdom (e.g., Heb 12:28), not as helping to build it. The work of constructing and expanding the kingdom belongs to God alone, and our response should simply be "gratitude and witness, not self-congratulation and ambitious social planning."[86]

---

82. Lumpkin, *Baptist Confessions of Faith*, 165. One can also find this language in the "True Confession" of 1596. Ibid., 87.

83. See Lumpkin's commentary on this confession. Ibid., 144–52.

84. Moore, *Kingdom of Christ*, 151–52.

85. Dargan, *Ecclesiology*, 537.

86. Horton, *Gospel Commission*, 244.

God advances his kingdom though the proclamation of the gospel, not through social action. He expands his kingdom when he draws a person to accept the gospel of Christ. Therefore, "good deeds are good, but they don't broaden the borders of the kingdom."[87] Revisionists simply err when they describe actions like feeding the hungry and cleaning the environment either as work that increases the kingdom.

Conclusion

The emerging church movement desires to effectively minister in the post-Christian, postmodern West. Leaders in the movement possess a commendable desire to engage the many non-Christians who live in the West, particularly those who have little contact with the Christian church. They use the term missional to describe their ministry efforts in our cultural context. Mark Driscoll believes he embraces the missional ethos by calling his church to view themselves as missionaries who contextualize the gospel and church life to the culture, and by extending his ministry through the multisite church model. One can commend much of Driscoll's ministry, though some concerns do merit attention. Revisionist leaders, however, typically embrace a model of missional living that conservative evangelicals, including many Baptists, will find troubling. One should avoid their understanding of the church's mission.

---

87. DeYoung and Gilbert, *What Is the Mission*, 121.

5

Assessing Emerging Church Leadership

STANLEY GRENZ HELPFULLY ILLUSTRATES the differences between postmodernity and modernity by offering an example drawn from American popular culture, the *Star Trek* television franchise.[1] In the original *Star Trek* series that aired during the 1960s, the character Spock was "the ideal Enlightenment man, completely rational and without emotion."[2] In many episodes, Spock solved problems for the crew of the *Enterprise* through his careful reasoning and lack of emotional attachment. The ship's captain, James Kirk, led with a strong personality and, in the words of Dan Kimball, was "always at the helm making decisions."[3] When the *Star Trek* franchise received an update for the 1990s, the writers brought in a new leadership paradigm. The ship's captain, Jean-Luc Picard, led more by consensus than fiat, and his ship's crew included a counselor, Troi, who could adeptly discover and develop the emotions of others.

1. Grenz, "Star Trek and the Next Generation," 24–32. Grenz expands on this work in Grenz, *Primer on Postmodernism*, 1–10. Dan Kimball makes use of Grenz's illustration in his work on church leadership. Kimball, *Emerging Church*, 229–30.

2. Grenz, "Star Trek and the Next Generation," 26.

3. Kimball, *Emerging Church*, 229.

Grenz explains that these differences symbolize the gap between modernity and postmodernity. Postmoderns typically have a strong distaste for authority figures or for those who exercise strong leadership styles.[4] Instead, they desire for emotional connections to develop within a group of people, and they desire for that group to make decisions as a close-knit community. Hence, the new *Star Trek* series illustrates well how the West's view of leadership has changed over the past several decades. It replaces the strong leadership of Kirk and the rationalism of Spock with the consensus building of Picard and the emotional connectedness of Counselor Troi.

All emerging leaders desire to reformulate church life in light of this postmodern shift. They each understand that postmoderns are suspicious of leadership and authority, but respond in differing ways. Revisionists propose leaderless groups in which church bodies collectively make decisions. More theologically conservative leaders speak of retaining traditional church leadership patterns but desire to explain them carefully given the postmodern context. For their part, reconstructionist leaders Frost and Hirsch endorse a rather interesting leadership model entitled APEPT. In this chapter, I will survey each of these emerging proposals and assess them from the viewpoint of a convictional Baptist. I will begin with a brief survey of Baptist convictions concerning church leadership, for these convictions will provide the evaluative tool for assessing emerging church proposals.

Leadership in Baptist Ecclesiology

As a people, Baptists have attained recognition primarily for their contributions to ecclesiology, and their ecclesiology has much to say in conversations related to decision-making and leadership within the church. In this section, I will briefly highlight four facets

---

4. James Sire notes that postmodern philosophers typically view claims of certainty as illegitimate grasps for power. This suspicion gives postmoderns a strong aversion to institutions and persons who have authority. Sire, *Universe Next Door*, 224–26.

of Baptist ecclesiology that relate to emerging church leadership proposals. I will give attention to principles historically affirmed by almost all Baptists.[5]

First, Baptists believe that Christ, and Christ alone, serves as the head of the church. The New Testament frequently refers to Christ's lordship and specifically mentions his lordship over the church in Colossians 1:15–20. Baptists argue that Christ should exercise final authority in the church, over and above the congregation and church leaders and even institutions outside of the church (such as associations or conventions). R. Stanton Norman explains, "As Baptists, we believe that the church exists under a Christocracy. Christ rules absolutely and immediately over those who belong to him."[6]

Second, Baptists practice congregational polity. As strong advocates of the doctrine of the priesthood of all believers, they believe regenerate church members are competent to direct the affairs of the church.[7] In a Baptist church, members in good standing may vote and participate in major church decisions. Some writers have noted that Baptists, by promoting this democratic form of church governance, model equality to a fallen and unjust world.[8]

Democracy within Baptist churches does have its limits, however. W. R. White reminds us, "In relation to Christ the church is not a democracy. It [the church] must be subject to his will as revealed in the New Testament and as experienced under the

---

5. Certainly not all Baptist churches function in the *exact* same manner. However, all share similar ecclesiological convictions.

6. Norman, *Baptist Way*, 41.

7. Competency certainly does not equate infallibility. Numerous congregations in Baptist history have unfortunately made erroneous decisions. However, the fact that congregations do sometimes err does not negate the correctness of congregational polity. See Dever, *Display of God's Glory*, 39–42.

8. B. H. Carroll explains that a Baptist church is a pure democracy and then writes, "Indeed, it is the only one [i.e., pure democracy] in the world. There is no disbarment of franchise on account of race, education, wealth, age, or sex. In Christ Jesus there is neither Jew nor Greek, barbarian, bond or free, man or woman or child. All its members are equal fellow-citizens, and the majority decides. It is of the people, for the people, by the people." Carroll, *Baptists and Their Doctrines*, 31.

guidance of the Holy Spirit."[9] Though members of the congregation have a voice in church affairs, they should base their decisions upon Christ and his leadership, not upon personal preference. John Hammett explains how Baptists reconcile Christ's lordship over the church with the practice of congregational polity by writing, "Christ exercises his headship through the members, as they all seek together to discern Christ's will for the body. Since all members are regenerate and thus indwelt by the Spirit, all are able to receive guidance from Christ."[10]

Third, Baptists believe that the church should maintain the scriptural offices of pastor (or elder) and deacon.[11] The function of the deacon varies in Baptist churches, and Scripture provides no exhaustive job description for this office. It merely indicates that deacons are servants (*diakonos*) of the church. Despite the importance of the office of deacon, I will not examine it at length in this work because it does not significantly pertain to emerging church conversations.[12] Here, I will focus his attention on the role of the pastor in Baptist life.

Regarding the office of pastor, Baptist history offers two distinct models of pastoral leadership. Some Baptists have advocated for a plurality of elders model.[13] Proponents of this model argue that sharing pastoral leadership among several pastors allows for wiser decision-making, greater accountability, and the sharing

9. White, *Baptist Distinctives*, 42.

10. Hammett, *Biblical Foundations for Baptist Churches*, 143.

11. The author believes the terms pastor and elder are synonymous and will use them interchangeably throughout this chapter. See Acts 20:17, 28 and 1 Pet 5:1–2. Numerous Baptist theologians also take this approach. See, for example, Dargan, *Ecclesiology*, 53–56; Grudem, *Systematic Theology*, 913–15; and Hammett, *Biblical Foundations*, 161–63.

12. Emerging literature rarely mentions the role of the deacon in church life. In addition, the New Testament indicates that the deacon is primarily to serve and not take on the primarily leadership role within the church. Therefore, the role of the deacon does not pertain to this chapter on church leadership patterns.

13. For a historical survey on the history of the plurality of elders model in Baptist history, see Dever, *By Whose Authority?* In addition, consider Newton, *Elders in Congregational Life*, 23–31.

Assessing Emerging Church Leadership

of ministry burdens.[14] Typically, churches operating within this model will consider all elders equal in leadership authority, though they may recognize one elder as the primary preaching pastor. Other Baptists eschew this collective leadership and argue that one man, the lead pastor, should provide leadership and direction for the church.[15] Most Baptist churches today appear to operate with the lead pastor model.

Regardless of which model a church employs, in Baptist thought the pastor (or elders) should lead, not rule, the congregation. While ultimate authority rests in the congregation as it submits to Christ (congregational polity), the congregation should follow the recognized leaders who meet the qualifications for elders given in 1 Timothy 3:1–7.[16] This fact typically means that Baptist congregations will entrust many church duties to the elder(s) of the church while retaining final say, under the guidance of the elders, in major issues like the admitting of members, the expulsion of members, and the calling of a new elder.

Given the rise of the feminist movement in the West, the gender of a church's elders has become a recent theological concern. Many evangelicals disagree on this issue, though most Baptists in the American context appear to have decided to restrict the office of pastor to men. This is evidenced by the fact that the Southern Baptist Convention, American's largest Protestant denomination (and thereby the largest Baptist denomination), recently updated its statement of faith to read, "While both men and women are gifted for service in the church, the office of pastor is limited to men as qualified by Scripture."[17] Baptists who promote this convic-

---

14. See the arguments regarding the benefits of the plurality of elders model in Merkle, *Why Elders?*, 43–60.

15. See Patterson, "Single-Elder-Congregationalism," 133–52; Akin, "Single-Elder-Led Church," 25–74.

16. Baptists attempt to balance Scripture's commands for congregational involvement and oversight (Acts 6:3; 1 Cor 5:2; 2 Cor 2:6; Matt 18:15–20) with the commands for elders to provide leadership in the church (Heb 13:7, 17; 1 Thess 5:12–13; 1 Tim 5:17–18).

17. Southern Baptist Convention, "Baptist Faith and Message 2000." For Southern Baptist writers who explain and defend this new wording, consider

tion do so not out of misogyny or a misplaced zeal for tradition, but rather out of a desire to obey their understanding of the New Testament's teachings regarding gender roles.[18]

Revisionists and Church Leadership

Criticism of Leadership Models of the Traditional Church

Emerging church leaders within the revisionist stream of the movement reflect postmodernity's suspicion towards authority and strong leadership. They offer stinging critiques of the traditional church, arguing that such churches place too much emphasis on a lead pastor who possesses authority over the rest of the congregation. Sally Morgenthaler, for example, refers to the traditional church as "the entrepreneurial church" because she believes it runs more like a modern business than a ministry organization.[19] She accuses traditional church leaders of serving more from the mindset of a CEO than of Christ. Tim Keel offers sentiments similar to Morgenthaler's, implying that in traditional church models leaders "dominate the environment" and reduce people "to mere pawns serving some larger agenda that comes from outside themselves."[20]

The Leaderless Model

Revisionists desire to create church leadership models that minimize the strong leadership they associate with the traditional church. They contend that churches today should become leaderless groups in order to encourage participation on the part of

---

White and White, "Offices and Women," 174–207.

18. A complementarian understanding of gender roles lies behind these efforts to restrict the office of pastor to men. Consider Piper and Grudem, *Recovering Biblical Manhood and Womanhood*.

19. Morgenthaler, "Leadership in a Flattened World," 181.

20. Keel, *Intuitive Leadership*, 112.

Assessing Emerging Church Leadership

everyone in the church body. Gibbs and Bolger believe this leaderless structure, sometimes referred to as leading as a body, is actually one of the key themes of the emerging church movement.[21] They write, "Leadership has shifted to a more facilitative role . . . the leader's role in such groups is to create a space for activities to occur."[22]

The term leaderless group can be slightly misleading. As Gibbs and Bolger clarify, "Leaderless groups do not advocate no leaders but simply that leadership be fluid, that all have a voice, that there be no named or appointed leader, and that leadership be flexible so that the right people lead the right things."[23] In such a model, rather than an appointed pastor or elder providing leadership for the church, the church body itself holds deliberations and decides collectively what to do.

Revisionist author Joseph Myers provides a good treatment of how such a construct might work.[24] He claims that modernity has supplied the traditional church with a "positional understanding of power."[25] He uses this phrase to refer to the fact that, in traditional leadership models, one's power and authority to lead emerges from the position and title that one holds. Myers believes that emerging organizations reject this model and instead operate with a revolving understanding of power. In this revolving model of power "positions have no place of permanent importance"[26] and the organization distributes leadership responsibilities depending on the tasks that need completion.

For example, should a church attender possess skills related to finance and the church face a financial difficulty, an emerging

21. Here the author will use the terms leaderless group and leadership by the body synonymously as they appear that way in much of emerging literature.

22. Gibbs and Bolger, *Emerging Churches*, 192.

23. Ibid., 198.

24. The Myers model fits well with what emerging writer Tim Keel has written on leadership. See Keel, *Intuitive Leadership*, 225–55. It also reflects Sally Morgenthaler's statements regarding leadership via collective intelligence. See Morgenthaler, "Leadership in a Flattened World," 178–79.

25. Myers, *Organic Community*, 97–98.

26. Ibid., 98.

church might recognize this person as an informal leader for a short season in order to provide direction in regards to the church's finances. This would happen spontaneously and unofficially of course and the entire church body would still have a large part in crafting the church's final decision. Once the financial troubles were over, however, the church might look to a different person to provide leadership related to a different need of the church. Myers entitles his model the revolving power paradigm because of this continual change in the unofficial leadership of the church.

The Leaderless Model and Female Leadership

Some revisionist leaders not only reject traditional church leadership patterns, but also express concern over the predominance of male leadership within the traditional church. Sally Morgenthaler argues many traditional churches follow a "great man with a great plan methodology"[27] by not only giving too much deference to the pastor, but by also insisting that the pastor should be male. She argues such a practice creates a patriarchal hierarchy within the church that minimizes the role of women.

Morgenthaler contends this minimization of women is unfortunate because, in her mind, women are more suited to function in postmodern culture than men. She believes that, in comparison to most men, women will be less likely to desire control and attention, making them right for the leaderless model. Rebecca Ver Straten-McSparran echoes Morgenthaler's sentiments by claiming that serving in the leaderless model allows her to serve with a distinctive "female way of doing things."[28] Though Morgenthaler and Ver Straten-McSparran offer the strongest calls for female involvement, other leaders in the revisionist stream of the emerging church movement also support calls for women to serve more openly in the ministry.[29]

---

27. Morgenthaler, "Leadership in a Flattened World," 187.

28. Testimony as recorded by Gibbs and Bolger. See Gibbs and Bolger, *Emerging Churches*, 209.

29. Stetzer notes many revisionists "are questioning (and in some cases

Assessing the Leaderless Model according to Baptist Ecclesiology

Baptists can acknowledge several positive features in the thought of these revisionist thinkers. Emerging church revisionists are right to speak against the leadership mistakes found in some traditional churches. Many churches unfortunately do not hold their leaders accountable and allow them to possess too much unchecked authority. A healthy involvement on the part of the congregation will help to prevent leadership abuses and provide necessary accountability.

In addition, Baptists can appreciate calls for congregational involvement because they have historically advocated for a congregational polity. Some revisionists have even started to recognize that similarities exist between the emerging church concept of leadership by the body and traditional congregational polity. In his most recent work, Tony Jones encourages emerging churches to "consider embracing a traditional Congregationalist polity in which each member is afforded one vote, clergy included."[30] This discussion by Jones helps to show Baptists, if nothing else, that they can emphasize their church's congregational polity as a way of removing obstacles that might prevent skeptical postmoderns from having an interest in the church.

However, though revisionist proposals possess some good qualities, the revisionist rejection of pastoral leadership should cause serious discomfort to Baptists. Proponents of the leaderless model are content to have unofficial leaders "organically" rise to serve the pressing needs of the congregation. By contrast, Baptists rightly emphasize that the congregation should allow certain members to consistently serve the church as officially recognized leaders. The influential Second London Confession speaks of some church members who are "gifted by the Holy Spirit unto the office

---

denying) issues like the nature of the substitutionary atonement, the reality of hell, *the complementarian nature of gender*, and the nature of the Gospel itself." Stetzer, "First-Person," n.p., emphasis added.

30. Jones, *Church Is Flat*, 169.

of Bishop, or Elder."[31] The New Testament teaches that this publically recognized office of elder carries with it certain leadership responsibilities.[32] Though emerging leaders do well to emphasize congregational involvement, in order to have a completely biblical view of church life, they should also be willing to accept the office of elder.

Revisionists will doubtlessly contend such a publicly recognized leadership office will hinder equality within the church. For example, citing Moltmann, Tony Jones argues for a social doctrine of the Trinity in which the persons of the Godhead dwell in an "eternal, mutually penetrating, and coequal relationship."[33] Jones rejects any notion that a hierarchy exists within the Trinity and believes we should model church life around this idea of a non-hierarchical, coequal relationship. In this line of thought, calling certain people to serve as recognized leaders within the church creates a hierarchy that upsets the coequal relationships the church should display.

Jones's proposal is deficient for a number of reasons, but here I wish only to note that behind it stands a false notion of equality. Jones appears to have a relational view of equality rather than an ontological one. That is, he defines one's value by the role he or she performs and not by one's intrinsic worth as an individual. If one submits to the leadership of another, then by default, in Jones's thinking, he or she has become inferior and a sinful hierarchy has begun.

Baptists should reject this false notion of equality because it does not square with Scripture. The members of the Trinity are certainly equal in every respect, yet a hierarchy exists among them in the sense that the Son willingly submits to the will of his Father.[34] It would be incorrect to argue that the Son's glad submission to the Father somehow robs him of his equality with the Father.

---

31. Second London Confession, as recorded in Lumpkin, *Baptist Confessions of Faith*, 287.

32. Consider texts such as Heb 13:7, 17; 1 Cor 16:16; and 1 Thess 5:12–13.

33. Jones, *Church Is Flat*, 167.

34. Feinberg, *No One Like Him*, 488.

Assessing Emerging Church Leadership

Therefore, even in the Godhead one sees that submission does not entail degradation. It is therefore possible for church members to submit to the leadership of other church members and retain their intrinsic worth as individuals.

Perhaps in an attempt to assuage some of the concerns emerging leaders such as Jones raise, Baptists should emphasize the fact that in congregational polity the congregation chooses its own leaders under Christ's direction. The aforementioned Second London Confession states elders are "chosen thereunto by the common suffrage of the church itself."[35] Pastoral leadership in a Baptist church therefore is not rule by an unwanted hierarchy. Rather, leaders in Baptist churches gain their positions because members of the congregation freely choose them based upon their character and desire to serve.

Finally, without clearly defined pastoral leadership, one must question the long-term viability of the leaderless model. People with dominant personalities will emerge who desire to direct the church's every decision. Such people will likely refuse to share power as emerging leaders advocate. In addition, given that all people are sinners, surely some people will eventually begin to ambitiously desire leadership in order to sinfully rule over others. One wonders how emerging churches will handle such difficulties. However, in the leaderless model, who will be responsible for carrying out church discipline or calling unrepentant leaders to account? While a publicly recognized elder board helps to provide some order in these situations, with no recognized leadership structure how will emerging churches prevent their communities from spiraling into anarchy?

Assessing the Leaderless Model and Female Leadership

Regarding the role of women in the church, clearly one's view on gender roles will guide this discussion. As the noted in the opening section, many Baptists espouse a complementarian understanding

---

35. Second London Confession. Lumpkin, *Baptist Confessions of Faith*, 287.

of gender roles. Complementarians would harbor serious objections to the dramatic calls for female leadership espoused by Morgenthaler and McSparran. Complementarian Baptists would argue that women can participate in many areas of the church's public worship gathering (see 1 Cor 11:5), but they would restrict the office of pastor to men. They would do so not out of misogyny or a desire to hold to traditional social customs, but because of texts such as 1 Timothy 2:11–15.

Regardless of one's stance on gender roles, however, all church leaders should be uncomfortable with Morgenthaler and McSparran's belief that the female gender will somehow be above power struggles and selfish ambition. Women indeed have a different psychological makeup than men. However, all humans, regardless of their sex, are depraved and are susceptible to the temptation to use their leadership gifts in an inappropriate manner.

Relevants and Traditional Church Leadership

Dan Kimball

Others leaders in the emerging church movement seek to retain more traditional church leadership patterns. Dan Kimball and Mark Driscoll are two well-known examples of such leaders. I will consider these two leaders separately, giving attention first to Kimball.

Kimball has no qualms with passages that instruct pastors to lead the church.[36] However, he does believe that pastors should minister with sensitivity given the suspicion many postmoderns have regarding leadership. He cites Jesus's admonition to be "as shrewd as snakes and as innocent as doves" as evidence that leaders, like shrewd snakes, should intelligently consider the cultural trends of their day while maintaining the purity commanded in

---

36. Kimball's church website explains, "In the context of Vintage Faith Church, there are leaders in our congregation, both paid and non-paid, who serve as 'pastors' in the way the Scriptures describes this term." Vintage Church, "Leadership at Vintage Church."

the Bible. In maintaining biblical purity, leaders remain as innocent as doves.[37]

Kimball instructs leaders operating within the traditional church model to make several modifications to their leadership style so they can wisely minister to postmoderns. Four of Kimball's suggested modifications are worthy of attention here, as these appear to be most important to him.[38] First, Kimball argues that church leaders should emphasize relationship over organization and structure. He writes, "We need to shift from a goals-driven leadership style to a relationship-driven style. We need to love people, not our goals and results."[39]

Second, Kimball believes the traditional church should eschew terminology commonly found in the business world, such as *management* team or *senior* pastor. According to Kimball, postmoderns will immediately associate such terminology with inauthenticity and organized religion.[40] Elsewhere, when describing the kind of leadership that postmoderns desire, he notes that, rather than a CEO, postmoderns crave leaders who are "poet-prophets, the rabbis, the philosophers who translate Scripture for this culture."[41] Rather than being impressed with efficient leadership structures, postmoderns desire leaders who point to a sense of transcendence and mystery.

Third, Kimball advises church leaders to include women in their public worship services as much as their theology will allow. He warns that some postmoderns perceive the church to be a male-dominated organization and hopes female participation will demonstrate to skeptical postmoderns that all have the opportunity

---

37. Kimball, *Emerging Church*, 238–41. Jesus makes this statement in Matt 10:16.

38. Kimball's most lengthy discussion of this appears in a chapter on leadership in his work entitled *Emerging Church*. These four themes receive constant mention in that chapter as well as in his work as a whole. See Kimball, *Emerging Church*, 213–25.

39. Ibid., 234.

40. Ibid., 213–25. Kimball notes that many postmoderns have a rather negative stereotype of organized religion.

41. Ibid., 232.

for service within Christ's church.[42] Fourth, he calls upon church leaders to carefully model humility and a teachable spirit. Kimball argues this will be especially attractive to postmoderns, as he notes that many of them believe arrogance and an unwillingness to listen have characterized the church in the past.[43]

Baptists should harbor no serious misgivings about these proposals. Kimball concerns himself with calling the church to humbly possess a concern for the sensitivities of others. Not only is such a thing wise, it is biblical. One could easily incorporate Kimball's suggestions into a Baptist church and not jeopardize historic Baptist ecclesiology. Conservative Baptists could even heed Kimball's call for greater female involvement in the worship time while retaining their complementarian convictions.[44]

Mark Driscoll

Like Kimball, Mark Driscoll desires to retain the biblical leadership roles. He rejects the postmodern protest against strong forms of leadership and calls for a plurality of male elders to direct the church.[45] Many Baptists will therefore find much in Driscoll's model they can commend: a call for robust church leadership, the use of the plurality of elders model, and the stipulation that only males can serve as elders within the church. Unfortunately, Driscoll also takes a strong stand against congregational church polity, believing it has no warrant in Scripture. He writes, "As I studied the Bible, I found more warrant for a church led by uni-

---

42. See Kimball, *They Like Jesus*, 115–35.

43. See Kimball's call for humble theology and ministry in Kimball, "Emerging Church and Missional Theology," 83–105. Also see Dan Kimball, "Humble Theology," 213–24.

44. Paul certainly envisions women praying and prophesying in a worship service in 1 Cor 11:5. Such a thing would not contradict Paul's instructions to ladies in other New Testament passages (e.g., 1 Tim 2:12–15).

45. Driscoll calls the postmodern protest against strong forms of leadership the "photocopy heresy." See Driscoll, *Radical Reformission*, 172–76. For Driscoll's views on church leadership, see Driscoll and Breshears, *Vintage Church*, 65–74.

Assessing Emerging Church Leadership

corns than by majority vote."⁴⁶ He also alleges that congregational polity is inefficient, warning "it has been proven statistically that while congregationally governed churches tend to have longevity, they cannot grow very large because they lack a clear leader."⁴⁷ In Driscoll's church, therefore, elders are akin to ruling elders and the congregation has much less voice than it would in a typical Baptist church.

Many popular Christian leaders today, who otherwise hold to Baptistic convictions about the church, have also decided to reject congregational polity.⁴⁸ There can be no doubt that sinful behavior on the part of some congregations has helped to inflame this opinion. Though Baptists know all too well of the difficulties sometimes found in congregationally led churches, they should not shy away from defending congregational polity for they believe Scripture reveals it to be God's plan for the church. Though no text explicitly states that churches *must* practice congregational governance, passages such as Acts 6:3, 1 Corinthians 5:2, 2 Corinthians 2:6, and Matthew 18:15–20 clearly speak of the congregation involving itself in such things as the selection of leaders, the acceptance and expulsion of members, and the process of church discipline. As Mark Dever writes, "The portrayal of congregationalism in the New Testament is quite an incomplete picture. We get it in snatches, asides, and assumptions. It is, however, clearly present, and the more one thinks about it, the more obvious it becomes throughout."⁴⁹

Furthermore, though Driscoll argues that congregational governance is inefficient and fraught with difficulty, in this

---

46. Driscoll, *Confessions of a Reformission Rev.*, 112. In addition, near the end of Driscoll's address at a recent missions conference, this author heard Driscoll speak about Baptist ecclesiology. Driscoll expressed appreciation for many historic Baptist convictions, but also insisted that Baptists should reject congregational polity because he deemed it inefficient and not Biblically sanctioned. See Driscoll, "Old Mission, New South."

47. Driscoll, *Confessions of a Reformission Rev.*, 103. Driscoll cites no source for this statement.

48. For example, MacDonald, "Congregational Government Is from Satan."

49. Dever, *Display of God's Glory*, 37–38.

author's mind the problems rest not with congregational governance but with the manner in which many churches carry it out. Inefficiency and difficulty typically emerge in congregational led churches when many in the congregation fail to properly submit their desires to the will of Christ. It would seem the solution for ending inefficiency in congregational polity, then, would not be to remove the practice all together, but to promote practices such as regenerate church membership and church discipline.[50] Practicing regenerate church membership and church discipline will help to ensure that only spiritual members who walk with Christ will have a voice or vote in church affairs.[51] Such a step will allow members to participate in their God-given right to participate in church affairs, but it can also minimize arguments and politicking in the life of the church.

While Baptists can appreciate some of what Driscoll offers, they should not follow him into a rejection of congregational polity. It is unfortunately true that many Baptist congregations today are inefficient and do not display a unity centered on Christ. However, Driscoll's proposed solution to this problem takes us, in Baptist thought, away from Scripture's teaching. Baptist pastors and elders should instead patiently work to reinstitute practices such as regenerate church membership and church discipline that will, in the long term, help to create a unified, Christ-following congregation.

---

50. If many members of the congregation are unregenerate or unspiritual, then taking a strong leadership stance would likely only compound the problems within the church, not weaken them. Unregenerate and unspiritual members would certainly have a difficult time submitting to strong leadership. For a helpful book on restoring the practices of regenerate membership and church discipline see White, Duesing, and Yarnell, *Restoring Integrity in Baptist Churches*.

51. Malcolm Yarnell offers a statement on the beauty of a healthy church that practices congregational polity. He notes, "Democracy is popularly understood in a more secular sense as a mere plurality." However, he goes on to write that Baptist democracy, a congregation banded together to follow Christ, "is best characterized by a filial consensus void of crass politics." Yarnell, "Article VI," 69n28.

Frost and Hirsch's APEPT Model

Introducing APEPT

Another model worthy of consideration to Baptists is the APEPT leadership model. In the emerging church movement, its most prominent proponents are the reconstructionists Michael Frost and Alan Hirsch.[52] The name APEPT comes from Ephesians 4:11, in which Paul mentions the ministries of apostles, prophets, evangelists, pastors, and teachers. Accordingly, APEPT serves as a simple acronym for the various ministry roles found in this Ephesians text.

Frost and Hirsch propose the APEPT model because they believe the traditional church has failed to grasp the importance of the differing ministries highlighted in Ephesians 4:11. They write, "We bemoan the current preference in churches for pastors and teachers at the exclusion of apostles, prophets, and evangelists . . . such a bias is a perversion of the Pauline idea."[53] To counter this perceived error, they instruct churches to form leadership teams deliberately made up of people that represent each of the ministries listed in Ephesians 4:11. They entitle this group of APEPT leaders the leadership matrix.[54]

Frost and Hirsch further allege that traditional church models, with their singular emphasis on pastors, are guilty of fostering a hierarchy within the church. Operating under this hierarchy, church attenders begin to feel as though ministry is merely the purview of those who hold a specific church office. Frost and Hirsch warn, "All Christians are ministers, but there will be no significant mission or ministry until we take that fact very seriously."[55] They believe APEPT will challenge all Christians, regardless of their office

---

52. The APEPT model is not unique to Frost and Hirsch, or even to the emerging church movement. Other well-known advocates include Wolfgang Simson and Peter Wagner. See Simson, *Houses That Change the World*; Wagner, *Apostles and Prophets*. Some authors refer to APEPT as "five-fold ministry."

53. Frost and Hirsch, *Shaping of Things to Come*, 172.

54. Ibid., 170.

55. Ibid., 172.

Baptists and the Emerging Church Movement

in the church, to view themselves as ministers. This is because the APEPT model instructs Christians they have been gifted by God in a specific way—apostle, prophet, evangelist, etc. Knowing they have received a ministry gift and calling, Christians will therefore be more likely to desire to minister within their local churches. Frost and Hirsch entitle church members operating according to their APEPT gifts the ministry matrix.[56]

In the Frost and Hirsch scheme, the church's leadership and members work together to fulfill the ministry roles listed in Ephesians 4:11. The office of pastor continues to exist (pastor is, after all, one of the offices listed in Eph 4:11), but a leadership team (leadership matrix) serves alongside the pastor in order to model differing APEPT ministries to the rest of the congregation. As the congregation, the ministry matrix, follows the direction of their leaders, they are equipped to undertake the APEPT ministries they feel called to perform because they see them modeled by their leaders. Frost and Hirsch explain, "No longer is the church run by pastors alone but by a developing APEPT leadership team whose aim is to help all the other ministers (everyone) to find their parts in the whole and pursue them."[57] The structure of Frost and Hirsch's APEPT church, then, is something akin to a community within a community. A community of leaders models APEPT ministries while the rest of the church performs APEPT ministries under the tutelage of these leaders.[58]

Assessing APEPT

Baptists can commend much in the APEPT model. They will certainly appreciate Frost and Hirsch's desire to place Scripture,

---

56. Ibid.

57. Ibid., *Shaping of Things to Come*, 173.

58. Frost and Hirsch write, "This is not to say that we are disregarding Paul's instructions for elders (or leaders) within the church. We see the leadership matrix as the community within the community, made up of certain people who are called to exemplify and embody these ministries in such a way as to be an APEPT leader to the rest of the APEPT body." Ibid., 172.

Assessing Emerging Church Leadership

Ephesians 4:11, at the center of their proposal. In addition, Baptists can appreciate how Frost and Hirsch desire to call all Christians to involve themselves in some form of ministry. The influential Second London Confession instructs all Christians that they are

> bound to maintain an holy fellowship and communion in the worship of God, and in performing such other spiritual services, as tend to their mutual edification; as also in relieving each other in outward things according to their several abilities, and necessities.[59]

This wording captures well the spirit of the New Testament. Each member should indeed view himself or herself as a gospel servant to others. The traditional church, in this author's mind, has been guilty of sometimes portraying Christian ministry as an office one holds rather than as a spiritual service all are to perform. Frost and Hirsch's proposal attempts to offer a helpful and necessary corrective.

However, for all of its merits, Frost and Hirsch's model should raise two concerns in the minds of Baptists. First, though Frost and Hirsch rightly attempt to draw their model from the Scripture, they base it entirely upon a single New Testament passage, Ephesians 4:11. Their model would have doubtlessly been more profitable if they had interacted with other New Testament passages that relate to church leadership. For example, some passages in the New Testament highlight the role of elders (pastors) in leading the church.[60] Though Frost and Hirsch certainly mention the work of pastors, they envision pastors leading the church alongside others gifted in differing APEPT skills (the leadership matrix). One wonders, then, if Frost and Hirsch give the pastorate the kind of primacy that Paul does. In texts related to church leadership, Paul does not mention those gifted as evangelists and prophets and apostles leading the local church alongside those who are gifted to

---

59. As recorded in Lumpkin, *Baptist Confessions of Faith*, 290.
60. Consider such texts as Titus 1:5-7; 1 Pet 5:1-2; Acts 20:17, 28.

be pastors. Instead, he explicitly connects the church's leadership to pastors alone.[61]

Second, Frost and Hirsch rightly view the Ephesians 4:11 ministries primarily as functions one performs rather than as public offices one holds. However, perhaps they go a bit too far in this line of thinking. Speaking of the ministry roles of Ephesians 4:11, they write, "Jesus's gracing of his church cannot be institutionalized into office."[62] In this author's mind, this statement reveals a false dichotomy. Though ministry is primarily a function one performs, this does not mean it cannot ever be a publically recognized office. Certainly he original apostles, whom Paul likely had in mind as he wrote the Ephesians 4:11 text, held some form of publicly recognized ministry office. In addition, the New Testament commands churches to publicly recognize those called as elders and to financially support them in their work.[63] Such commands appear to point to some form of publicly recognized ministry office. While Frost and Hirsch are right to criticize the traditional church for sometimes representing ministry as *merely* an office, they are wrong to imply a church is wrong to ever institutionalize a publicly recognized ministry office.

Conclusion

Emerging leaders offer a range of proposals related to church leadership. Revisionists call for a leaderless model that will simply be incompatible with much of Baptist ecclesiology. Relevants such as Kimball and Driscoll offer attractive proposals that seek to uphold the leadership structures present in most traditional churches,

---

61. Baptists who believe in a plurality of elders could overcome this problem by simply calling believers who possess a variety of spiritual gifts to serve as elders. In this way, they can take advantage of the kind of diversity that Frost and Hirsch advocate while also maintaining the New Testament's expectation that elders lead the church.

62. Frost and Hirsch, *Shaping of Things to Come*, 168.

63. See the Second London Confession's statement on this as well as the Scripture citations that it offers. Lumpkin, *Baptist Confessions of Faith*, 287.

though Driscoll does unfortunately oppose congregational governance. Frost and Hirsch's interesting APEPT model represents a healthy desire to follow Scripture's teaching regarding church leadership. With some adjustments, Baptists could use some of its insights in their churches.

Conclusion

EMERGING CHURCH LEADERS BELIEVE that Western culture has experienced a profound philosophical shift toward postmodernity over the past several years. They have a commendable desire to reach those on the front line of this cultural shift with the message of Christianity. They propose changes to traditional church ecclesiology in order to make church life appealing and understandable to those raised in the new postmodern ethos. Some of their suggestions are positive and Baptists can embrace such proposals and learn from them. However, Baptists should reject many of the proposals that originate from the revisionist and, at times, reconstructionist streams of the movement, because many of these proposals are incompatible with historic Baptist ecclesiology.

Bibliography

Akin, Daniel L. "The Single-Elder-Led Church: The Bible's Witness to a Congregational/Single Elder-Led Polity." In *Perspectives on Church Government*, edited by Chad Owen Brand and R. Stanton Norman, 25–74. Nashville: Broadman & Holman, 2004.

Anderson, Ray. *An Emergent Theology for Emerging Churches*. Downers Grove: InterVarsity, 2006.

Armstrong, Chris. "The Future Lies in the Past." *Christianity Today* 52 (2008) 22–29.

Avis, Paul. *The Church in the Theology of the Reformers*. Eugene, OR: Wipf & Stock, 2002.

Belcher, Jim. *Deep Church: A Third Way beyond Emerging and Traditional*. Downers Grove: InterVarsity, 2009.

Bell, Rob. *Velvet Elvis: Repainting the Christian Faith*. Grand Rapids: Zondervan, 2005.

Best, Harold. "Emerging Worship: A Traditional Worship Response." In *Six Views on Exploring the Worship Spectrum*, edited by Paul A. Basden, 233–37. Grand Rapids: Zondervan, 2004.

Blomberg, Craig. *Contagious Holiness: Jesus' Meals with Sinners*. Downers Grove: InterVarsity, 2005.

Bohannon, John. "Preaching and the Emerging Church: An Examination of Four Founding Leaders: Mark Driscoll, Dan Kimball, Brian McLaren, and Doug Pagitt." PhD diss., Southeastern Baptist Theological Seminary, 2010.

Bosch, David. *Transforming Mission: Paradigm Shifts in Theology of Mission*. Maryknoll: Orbis, 1991.

Bradley, Anthony. "Farewell Emerging Church, 1989–2010." *World*. April 14, 2010. No pages. http://www.worldmag.com/2010/04/farewell_emerging_church_1989_2010.

Brewer, Paul. "Embracing God's Word in Worship." *Baptist History and Heritage* 27 (1992) 13–22.

Brewin, Kester. *Signs of Emergence: A Vision for Church That Is Organic. . . .* Grand Rapids: Baker, 2007.

Bibliography

Burke, Spencer. "From the Third Floor to the Garage." In *Stories of Emergence: Moving From Absolute to Authentic*, edited by Mike Yaconelli, 27–39. Grand Rapids: Zondervan, 2003.

Canosa, Amy. "I Pledge Allegiance to the Kingdom." In *Baptimergent: Baptist Stories from the Emergent Frontier*, edited by Zach Roberts, 141–49. Macon, GA: Smyth & Helwys, 2010.

Carroll, B. H. *Baptists and Their Doctrines: Sermons on Distinctive Baptist Principles*. Compiled by J. B. Cranfill. Chicago: Revell, 1913.

Carson, D. A. *Becoming Conversant with the Emerging Church: Understanding a Movement and Its Implications*. Grand Rapids: Zondervan, 2005.

———. *The Gagging of God: Christianity Confronts Pluralism*. Grand Rapids: Zondervan, 1996.

Celek, Tim, et al. *Inside the Soul of a New Generation: Insights and Strategies for Reaching Busters*. Grand Rapids: Zondervan, 1996.

Challies, Tim. Review of *Real Marriage*, by Mark Driscoll and Grace Driscoll. Tim Challies's blog. January 2, 2012. No pages. http://www.challies.com/book-reviews/book-review-real-marriage.

Clark, Neville. *Call to Worship*. London: SCM, 1960.

Conder, Tim. *The Church in Transition: The Journey of Existing Churches into Emerging Culture*. Grand Rapids: Zondervan, 2006.

———. "The Existing Church/Emerging Church Matrix." In *An Emergent Manifesto of Hope*, edited by Doug Pagitt and Tony Jones, 97–107. Grand Rapids: Baker, 2007.

Corcoran, Kevin, ed. *Church in the Present Tense: A Candid Look at What's Emerging*. Grand Rapids: Brazos, 2011.

Craigen, Trevor. "Emergent Soteriology: The Dark Side." *Master's Seminary Journal* 17 (2006) 177–90.

Cyprian. *The Lapsed; On the Unity of the Catholic Church*. Translated by Maurice Bevenot. Westminster: Newman, 1957.

Dargan, Edwin Charles. *Ecclesiology: A Study of the Churches*. Louisville: Dearing, 1905.

Dever, Mark. *By Whose Authority? Elders in Baptist Life*. Washington, DC: 9Marks, 2006.

———. *A Display of God's Glory: Basics of Church Structure*. Washington, DC: 9Marks, 2001.

———. "Regaining Meaningful Church Membership." In *Restoring Integrity in Baptist Churches*, edited by Thomas White et al., 45–61. Grand Rapids: Kregel, 2008.

Dever, Mark, and Paul Alexander. *The Deliberate Church: Building Your Ministry on the Gospel*. Wheaton, IL: Crossway, 2005.

Devine, Mark. "The Emerging Church: One Movement—Two Streams." In *Evangelicals Engaging Emergent*, edited by William D. Henard and Adam W. Greenway, 4–46. Nashville: Broadman & Holman, 2009.

Deweese, Charles W. *Baptist Church Covenants*. Nashville: Broadman, 1990.

Bibliography

DeYoung, Kevin, and Greg Gilbert. *What Is the Mission of the Church?* Wheaton, IL: Crossway, 2011.

DeYoung, Kevin, and Ted Kluck. *Why We Love the Church*. Chicago: Moody, 2009.

———. *Why We're Not Emergent: By Two Guys Who Should Be*. Chicago: Moody, 2008.

Dockery, David. *Southern Baptist Consensus and Renewal*. Nashville: Broadman & Holman, 2008.

Douthat, Ross. *Bad Religion: How We Became a Nation of Heretics*. New York: Free Press, 2012.

Downing, Crystal. *How Postmodernism Serves (My) Faith*. Downers Grove: InterVarsity, 2006.

Driscoll, Mark. "The Church and the Supremacy of Christ." In *The Supremacy of Christ in a Postmodern World*, edited by John Piper and Justin Taylor, 125–48. Wheaton, IL: Crossway, 2007.

———. *Confessions of a Reformission Rev.: Hard Lessons from an Emerging Missional Church*. Grand Rapids: Zondervan, 2006.

———. "The Emerging Church and Biblicist Theology." In *Listening to the Beliefs of Emerging Churches*, edited by Robert Webber, 21–47. Grand Rapids: Zondervan, 2007.

———. "How Sharp the Edge? Christ, Controversy, and Cutting Words." Conference message, with session notes. September 27, 2008. *Desiring God.org*. Video, 1 hr. 22 mins. http://www.desiringgod.org/conference-messages/how-sharp-the-edge-christ-controversy-and-cutting-words.

———. "Old Mission, New South." Sermon given at Advance the Church 2010, Durham, NC, April 26, 2010. https://itunes.apple.com/us/podcast/advance-the-church/id370705699?mt=2.

———. "A Pastoral Perspective on the Emerging Church." *Criswell Theological Review*, n.s., 3 (2006) 87–93.

———. *Radical Reformission: Reaching Out without Selling Out*. Grand Rapids: Zondervan, 2004.

———. *Religion Saves and Nine Other Misconceptions*. Wheaton, IL: Crossway, 2009.

———. "Response to Karen Ward." In *Listening to the Beliefs of Emerging Churches*, edited by Robert Webber, 183–86. Grand Rapids: Zondervan, 2007.

Driscoll, Mark, and Gerry Breshears. *Vintage Church: Timeless Truths and Timely Methods*. Wheaton, IL: Crossway, 2008.

———. *Doctrine: What Christians Should Believe*. Wheaton, IL: Crossway, 2010.

Driscoll, Mark, and Grace Driscoll. *Real Marriage: The Truth about Sex, Friendship & Life Together*. Nashville: Thomas Nelson, 2012.

Economist Staff. "Christian Festivals: A Broader Church." *Economist* 399 (2011) 26.

Bibliography

Emergent Village. "Rick McKinley Shares His Thoughts on the Emerging Church." No pages. http://www.emergentvillage.com/weblog/rick-mckinley-shares-his-thoughts-on-the-emerging-church.

Feinberg, John. *No One Like Him: The Doctrine of God*. Wheaton, IL: Crossway, 2001.

Finn, Nathan. A. "A Historical Analysis of Church Membership." In *Those Who Must Give Account: A Study of Church Membership and Church Discipline*, edited by John S. Hammett and Benjamin L. Merkle, 53–79. Nashville: Broadman & Holman, 2012.

Frost, Michael, and Alan Hirsch. *The Shaping of Things to Come: Innovation and Mission for the 21st Century*. Peabody, MA: Hendrickson, 2003.

Frye, Brian Nathaniel. "The Multi-Site Church Phenomenon in North America: 1950–2010." PhD diss., Southern Baptist Theological Seminary, 2011.

Gaines, Grant. "Exegetical Critique of Multi-Site: Disassembling the Church?" *9Marks*, May/June 2009, no pages. http://www.9marks.org/ejournal/exegetical-critique-multi-site-disassembling-church.

Gibbs, Eddie, and Ryan K. Bolger. *Emerging Churches: Creating Christian Community in Postmodern Cultures*. Grand Rapids: Baker, 2005.

Gilley, Gary. *This Little Church Stayed Home: A Faithful Church in Deceptive Times*. Webster, NY: Evangelical, 2006.

Grenz, Stanley. *A Primer on Postmodernism*. Grand Rapids: Eerdmans, 1996.

―――. "Star Trek and the Next Generation: Postmodernism and the Future of Evangelical Theology." *Crux* 30 (1994) 24–32.

Grudem, Wayne. *Systematic Theology*. Grand Rapids: Zondervan, 2000.

Guder, Darrell. *The Continuing Conversion of the Church*. Grand Rapids: Eerdmans, 2000.

―――, ed. *Missional Church: A Vision for the Sending of the Church in North America*. Grand Rapids: Eerdmans, 1998.

―――. "The Missional Church: From Sending to Being Sent." In *Missional Church*, 1–17. Grand Rapids: Eerdmans, 1998.

Hammett, John. *Biblical Foundations for Baptist Churches: A Contemporary Ecclesiology*. Grand Rapids: Kregel, 2005.

―――. "The Church according to Emergent/Emerging Church." In *Evangelicals Engaging Emergent*, edited by William D. Henard and Adam W. Greenway, 219–60. Nashville: Broadman & Holman, 2009.

―――. "Regenerate Church Membership." In *Restoring Integrity in Baptist Churches*, edited by Thomas White et al., 21–43. Grand Rapids: Kregel, 2010.

―――. "What Makes a Multi-Site Church One Church?" Paper presented at the annual meeting of the Evangelical Theological Society, San Francisco, November 17, 2011.

Hansen, Collin. "Pastor Provocateur." *Christianity Today* 51 (2007) 44–49.

―――. *Young, Restless, and Reformed: A Journalist's Journey with the New Calvinists*. Wheaton, IL: Crossway, 2008.

Bibliography

Harris, Josh. "Desiring God 2006: Day Two." Joshua Harris's blog. September 30, 2006. No pages. http://joshharrisblogson.blogspot.com/2006/10/desiring-god-2006-day-two.html.

Haykin, Michael. Review of *Finding Our Way Again: The Return of Ancient Practices* by Brian McLaren. *Southern Baptist Journal of Theology* 12 (2008) 62–67.

Hellerman, Joseph. *When the Church Was a Family: Recapturing Jesus' Vision for Authentic Community*. Nashville: Broadman & Holman, 2009.

Hiebert, Paul. *Anthropological Reflections on Missiological Issues*. Grand Rapids: Baker, 1994.

Hill, Jonathan. *What Has Christianity Ever Done for Us? How It Shaped the Modern World*. Downers Grove: InterVarsity, 2005.

Holland, Richard. "Progressional Dialogue and Preaching: Are They the Same?" *Master's Seminary Journal* 17 (2006) 207–22.

Horton, Michael. "Better Homes & Gardens." In *The Church in Emerging Culture: Five Perspectives*, edited by Leonard Sweet, 105–25. Grand Rapids: Zondervan, 2003.

———. *The Gospel Commission: Recovering God's Strategy for Making Disciples*. Grand Rapids: Baker, 2011.

Hughes, R. Kent. "Free Church Worship: The Challenge of Freedom." In *Worship by the Book*, edited by D. A. Carson, 136–92. Grand Rapids: Zondervan, 2002.

Hunter, George, III. *The Celtic Way of Evangelism: How Christianity Can Reach the West Again*. Nashville: Abingdon, 2000.

Irenaeus of Lyons. *Against the Heresies*. Translated by Dominic Unger. New York: Newman, 2012.

Johnson, Phil. "Joyriding on the Downgrade at Breakneck Speed: The Dark Side of Diversity." In *Reforming or Conforming: Post-Conservative Evangelicals and the Emerging Church*, edited by Gary L. W. Johnson and Ronald N. Gleason, 211–23. Wheaton, IL: Crossway, 2008.

Jones, Andrew. "Ed Stetzer Gets It." *Tall Skinny Kiwi* (blog), January 8, 2006. No pages. http://tallskinnykiwi.typepad.com/tallskinnykiwi/2006/01/ed_stetzer_gets.html.

———. "Emerging Church Movement (1989–2009)?" *Tall Skinny Kiwi* (blog), December 30, 2009. No pages. http://tallskinnykiwi.typepad.com/tallskinnykiwi/2009/12/emerging-church-movement-1989—-2009.html.

———. "The 50 Books on My Emerging Church Bookshelf." *Tall Skinny Kiwi* (blog), June 14, 2006. No pages. http://tallskinnykiwi.typepad.com/tallskinnykiwi/2006/06/the_50_books_on.html.

Jones, Tony. *The Church Is Flat: The Relational Ecclesiology of the Emerging Church Movement*. Minneapolis: JoPa, 2011.

———. "Friendship, Faith, and Going Somewhere Together." In *An Emergent Manifesto of Hope*, edited by Doug Pagitt and Tony Jones, 11–15. Grand Rapids: Baker, 2007.

Bibliography

———. *The New Christians: Dispatches from the Emergent Frontier.* San Francisco: Jossey-Bass, 2008.

———. *The Sacred Way: Spiritual Practices for Everyday Life.* Grand Rapids: Zondervan, 2005.

Keel, Tim. *Intuitive Leadership: Embracing a Paradigm for Narrative, Metaphor, and Chaos.* Grand Rapids: Baker, 2007.

Kelly, Mark. "Driscoll's Vulgarity Draws Media Attention." *Baptist Press*, May 11, 2009. No pages. http://www.bpnews.net/bpnews.asp?id=35091.

Kimball, Dan. "The Emerging Church and Missional Theology." In *Listening to the Beliefs of the Emerging Church*, edited by Robert Webber, 81–105. Grand Rapids: Zondervan, 2007.

———. *The Emerging Church: Vintage Christianity for New Generations.* Grand Rapids: Zondervan, 2003.

———. "Emerging Worship." In *Perspectives on Christian Worship: Five Views*, edited by J. Matthew Pinson, 288–333. Nashville: Broadman & Holman, 2009.

———. *Emerging Worship: Creating New Worship Gatherings for Emerging Generations.* Grand Rapids: Zondervan, 2004.

———. "Emerging Worship: Moving beyond Preaching and Singing." *Clergy Journal* 83 (2006) 8–10.

———. "Humble Theology: Re-Exploring Doctrine while Holding On to Truth." In *An Emergent Manifesto of Hope*, edited by Doug Pagitt and Tony Jones, 213–24. Grand Rapids: Baker, 2007.

———. *They Like Jesus but Not the Church: Insights from Emerging Generations.* Grand Rapids: Zondervan, 2007.

Kimball, Dan, and Lilly Lewin. *Sacred Space: A Hands-On Guide to Creating Multisensory Worship Experiences for Youth Ministry.* Grand Rapids: Zondervan, 2008.

Ladd, George Eldon. *A Theology of the New Testament.* Rev. ed. Edited by Donald Hagner. Grand Rapids: Eerdmans, 2000.

Leeman, Jonathan. *The Church and the Surprising Offense of God's Love.* Wheaton, IL: Crossway, 2010.

———. *Reverberation: How God's Word Brings Light, Freedom, and Action to His People.* Chicago: Moody, 2011.

———. "What Is the Missional Church?" October 2006. No pages. http://sites.silaspartners.com/cc/article/0,,PTID314526_CHID598014_CIID2265778,00.html.

Liederbach, Mark, and Alvin Reid. *The Convergent Church: Missional Worshippers in an Emerging Culture.* Grand Rapids: Kregel, 2009.

Lumpkin, William, ed. *Baptist Confessions of Faith.* Rev. ed. Valley Forge, PA: Judson, 1969.

MacArthur, John. "Grunge Christianity?" *Grace to You* website. December 11, 2006. No pages. http://www.gty.org/Resources/articles/2643.

Bibliography

MacDonald, James. "Congregational Government Is from Satan." No pages. http://theelephantsdebt.files.wordpress.com/2012/06/congregational-government-is-from-satan.pdf.
McBeth, Leon. *The Baptist Heritage: Four Centuries of Baptist Witness*. Nashville: Broadman, 1987.
McConnell, Scott. *Multi-Site Churches: Guidance for the Movement's Next Generation*. Nashville: Broadman & Holman, 2009.
McCracken, Brett. "The Church in a 'Missional' Age." *Biola Magazine*, Spring 2009. No pages. http://magazine.biola.edu/article/09-spring/the-church-in-a-missional-age/.
———. *Hipster Christianity: When Church and Cool Collide*. Grand Rapids: Baker, 2010.
McLaren, Brian. *Everything Must Change: Jesus, Global Crises, and a Revolution of Hope*. Nashville: Nelson, 2007.
———. "Everything Old Is New Again." *Sojourners* 38 (2009) 23–25.
———. *Finding Our Way Again: The Return of the Ancient Practices*. Nashville: Nelson, 2008.
———. *A Generous Orthodoxy*. Grand Rapids: Zondervan, 2004.
———. "The Method, the Message, and the Ongoing Story." In *The Church in Emerging Culture: Five Perspectives*, edited by Leonard Sweet, 191–230. Grand Rapids: Zondervan, 2003.
———. *More Ready than You Realize: Evangelism as Dance in the Postmodern Matrix*. Grand Rapids: Zondervan, 2006.
———. *A New Kind of Christian: A Tale of Two Friends on a Spiritual Journey*. San Francisco: Jossey-Bass, 2001.
———. *The Secret Message of Jesus: Uncovering the Truth That Could Change Everything*. Nashville: Thomas Nelson, 2007.
———. *The Story We Find Ourselves In: Further Adventures of a New Kind of Christian*. San Francisco: Jossey-Bass, 2003.
McLaren, Brian, and Tony Campolo. *Adventures in Missing the Point: How the Culture-Controlled Church Neutered the Gospel*. Grand Rapids: Zondervan, 2003.
McKibbens, Thomas, Jr. "Our Baptist Heritage in Worship." *Review and Expositor* 80 (1983) 53–69.
McKinley, Mike. *Church Planting Is for Wimps: How God Uses Messed-Up People to Plant Ordinary Churches That Do Extraordinary Things*. Wheaton, IL: Crossway, 2010.
McKnight, Scot. "Five Streams of the Emerging Church." *Christianity Today* 51 (2007) 34–39.
———. "What Is the Emerging Church?" Paper presented at Fall Contemporary Issues Conference, Westminster Theological Seminary, Philadelphia, October 26–27, 2006.
Merkle, Benjamin. *Why Elders? A Biblical and Practical Guide for Church Members*. Grand Rapids: Kregel, 2009.

Bibliography

Miles, Todd. "A Kingdom without a King? Evaluating the Kingdom Ethic(s) of the Emerging Church." *Southern Baptist Journal of Theology* 12 (2008) 88–103.

Millar, Gary. "A Biblical Theology of Mission: An Evaluation of Chris Wright." Audio recording, 1 hr. 2 mins. April 7, 2013. Gospel Coalition 2013 National Conference. http://thegospelcoalition.org/resources/entry/a_biblical_theology_of_mission_an_evaluation_of_chris_wright.

Miller, Donald. *Blue Like Jazz: Nonreligious Thoughts on Christian Spirituality*. Nashville: Nelson, 2003.

Mohler, R. Albert, Jr. *He Is Not Silent: Preaching in a Postmodern World*. Chicago: Moody, 2008.

———. "The Primacy of Preaching." In *Feed My Sheep: A Passionate Plea for Preaching*, edited by Don Kistler, 1–17. Orlando: Reformation Trust, 2008.

Moore, Russell. *The Kingdom of Christ: The New Evangelical Perspective*. Wheaton, IL: Crossway, 2004.

Morgenthaler, Sally. "Emerging Worship." In *Exploring the Worship Spectrum: Six Views*, edited by Paul A. Basden, 215–30. Grand Rapids: Zondervan, 2004.

———. "Leadership in a Flattened World: Grassroots Culture and the Demise of the CEO Model." In *An Emergent Manifesto of Hope*, edited by Doug Pagitt and Tony Jones, 175–88. Grand Rapids: Baker, 2007.

Mouw, Richard J. "Carl Henry Was Right." *Christianity Today* 54 (2010) 30–33.

Moynagh, Michael. *EmergingChurch.Intro: Fresh Expressions of Church, Examples That Work, the Big Picture, What You Can Do*. Grand Rapids: Monarch, 2004.

Murray, Stuart. *Church after Christendom*. Colorado Springs: Paternoster, 2004.

———. *Post-Christendom: Church and Mission in a Strange New World*. Colorado Springs: Paternoster, 2004.

Myers, Joseph. *Organic Community: Creating a Place Where People Naturally Connect*. Grand Rapids: Baker, 2007.

Nelson, Gary. "Everything Old Is New Again: Emerging Church Ecclesiology." Paper presented at the Baptist World Alliance Symposium, Elstal, Germany, March 2007.

Newbigin, Lesslie. *The Open Secret: An Introduction to the Theology of Mission*. Grand Rapids: Eerdmans, 1995.

Newton, Phil. *Elders in Congregational Life: Rediscovering the Biblical Model for Church Leadership*. Grand Rapids: Kregel, 2005.

Norman, R. Stanton. *The Baptist Way: Distinctives of a Baptist Church*. Nashville: Broadman & Holman, 2005.

———. *More than Just a Name: Preserving Our Distinctive Baptist Identity*. Nashville: Broadman & Holman, 2001.

———. "A Southern Baptist Identity: A Theological Perspective." In *Southern Baptist Identity*, edited by David S. Dockery, 43–63. Wheaton, IL: Crossway, 2009.

Bibliography

Pagitt, Doug. *Church Re-Imagined: The Spiritual Formation of People in Communities of Faith*. Grand Rapids: Zondervan, 2005.

———. *Preaching Re-Imagined: The Role of the Sermon in Communities of Faith*. Grand Rapids: Zondervan, 2005.

Patterson, Paige. "Single-Elder Congregationalism." In *Who Runs the Church? 4 Views on Church Government*, edited by Steven B. Cowan, 133–52. Grand Rapids: Zondervan, 2004.

Pearcey, Nancy. *Saving Leonardo*. Nashville: Broadman & Holman, 2010.

Petersen, Jim. *Church without Walls: Moving beyond Traditional Boundaries*. Colorado Springs: NavPress, 1992.

Piper, John, and Wayne Grudem, eds. *Recovering Biblical Manhood and Womanhood*. Wheaton, IL: Crossway, 1991.

Plummer, Robert. *Paul's Understanding of the Church's Mission*. Waynesboro, GA: Paternoster, 2006.

Preaching Magazine. "Preaching in the Emerging Church: An Interview with Dan Kimball." *Preaching* 20 (2004) 6–9, 48–51.

Putnam, Robert. *Bowling Alone: The Collapse and Revival of American Community*. New York: Simon & Schuster, 2000.

Renihan, James M. *Edification and Beauty: The Practical Ecclesiology of the English Particular Baptists, 1675–1705*. Eugene, OR: Wipf & Stock, 2008.

Richardson, Rick. *Reimagining Evangelism: Inviting Friends on a Spiritual Journey*. Downers Grove: InterVarsity, 2006.

Rollins, Peter. *How (Not) to Speak of God*. Brewster: Paraclete, 2006.

———. "Transformation Art: Reconfiguring the Social Self." In *Church in the Present Tense: A Candid Look at What's Emerging*, by Scot McKnight et al., 89–102. Grand Rapids: Brazos, 2011.

Schmidt, Alvin J. *How Christianity Changed the World*. Grand Rapids: Zondervan, 2004.

Simson, Wolfgang. *Houses That Change the World: The Return of the House Churches*. Waynesboro, GA: Authentic, 2001.

Sire, James. *The Universe Next Door: A Basic Worldview Catalogue*. 5th ed. Downers Grove: InterVarsity, 2009.

Slaughter, Mike. *Change the World: Recovering the Message and Mission of Jesus*. Nashville: Abingdon, 2010.

Smith, James K. A. "The Emerging Church." *Reformed Worship* 77 (2005) 40–41.

Smith, R. Scott. *Truth and the New Kind of Christian: The Emerging Effects of Postmodernism in the Church*. Wheaton, IL: Crossway, 2005.

Southern Baptist Convention. "Baptist Faith and Message 2000." No pages. http://www.sbc.net/bfm2000/bfm2000.asp.

Springer, Laura. "Hunting for Taxonomies." *Who in the World Are We* (blog), January 15, 2008. No pages. http://whointheworldarewe.blogspot.com/2008/01/hunting-for-taxonomies.html.

Bibliography

Stetzer, Ed. "First-Person: Understanding the Emerging Church." *Baptist Press*, January 6, 2006. No pages. http://www.sbcbaptistpress.org/bpnews.asp?ID=22406.

———. "Interview with Mark Driscoll." *Acts 29 Network*. No pages. http://www.acts29network.org/acts-29-blog/interview-with-mark-driscoll-by-dr-ed-stetzer/. Link no longer accessible.

Stetzer, Ed, and David Putman. *Breaking the Missional Code*. Nashville: Broadman & Holman, 2006.

Stott, John. *Christian Mission in the Modern World*. Downers Grove: InterVarsity, 1975.

Surratt, Geoff, et al. *The Multi-Site Church Revolution: Being One Church in Many Locations*. Grand Rapids: Zondervan, 2006.

———. *Multi-Site Road Trip: Exploring the New Normal*. Grand Rapids: Zondervan, 2009.

Sweet, Leonard. *The Gospel according to Starbucks: Living with a Grande Passion*. Colorado Springs: WaterBrook, 2007.

———. *Post-Modern Pilgrims: First Century Passion for the 21st Century World*. Nashville: Broadman & Holman, 2000.

Tickle, Phyllis. *The Great Emergence: How Christianity Is Changing and Why*. Grand Rapids: Baker, 2008.

Towns, Elmer, and Ed Stetzer. *Perimeters of Light: Biblical Boundaries for the Emerging Church*. Chicago: Moody, 2004.

Tu, Janet I. "Pastor Mark Packs 'Em In." *Seattle Times*, November 30, 2003. No pages. http://seattletimes.nwsource.com/pacificnw/2003/1130/cover.html.

Wagner, C. Peter. *Apostles and Prophets: The Foundation of the Church*. Ventura, CA: Regal, 2002.

Wamble, Hugh. "The Concept and Practice of Christian Fellowship: The Connectional and Inter-Denominational Aspects Thereof, among Seventeenth Century English Baptists." ThD diss., Southern Baptist Theological Seminary, 1955.

Ward, Karen. "The Emerging Church and Communal Theology." In *Listening to the Beliefs of Emerging Churches: Five Perspectives*, edited by Robert Webber, 161–82. Grand Rapids: Zondervan, 2007.

Ward, Pete. *Liquid Church*. Peabody, MA: Hendrickson, 2002.

Wells, David. *The Courage to Be Protestant: Truth-Lovers, Marketers, and Emergents in the Postmodern World*. Grand Rapids: Eerdmans, 2008.

White, Thomas, Jason G. Duesing, and Malcolm B. Yarnell, eds. *Restoring Integrity in Baptist Churches*. Grand Rapids: Kregel, 2008.

White, Thomas, and Joy White. "The Offices and Women: Can Women Be Pastors? Or Deacons?" In *Upon This Rock: The Baptist Understanding of the Church*, by Jason G. Duesing et al., 174–207. Nashville: Broadman & Holman, 2010.

White, Thomas, and John Yeats. *Franchising McChurch: Feeding Our Obsession with Easy Christianity*. Colorado Springs: Cook, 2009.

White, W. R. *Baptist Distinctives*. Nashville: Sunday Board of the Southern Baptist Convention, 1946.
Whitley, W. T., ed. *The Works of John Smyth*. New York: Cambridge University Press, 1915.
Worthen, Molly. "Who Would Jesus Smack Down?" *New York Times Magazine*, January 6, 2009. http://www.nytimes.com/2009/01/11/magazine/11punk-t.html?pagewanted=all.
Wright, Christopher J. H. *The Mission of God: Unlocking the Bible's Grand Narrative*. Downers Grove: InterVarsity, 2006.
———. *The Mission of God's People: A Biblical Theology of the Church's Mission*. Grand Rapids: Zondervan, 2010.
Yarnell, Malcolm B., III. "Article VI: The Church." In *Baptist Faith and Message 2000: Critical Issues in America's Largest Protestant Denomination*, edited by Douglas K. Blount and Joseph D. Wooddell, 55–70. Lanham, MD: Rowan & Littlefield, 2007.

www.ingramcontent.com/pod-product-compliance
Lightning Source LLC
Chambersburg PA
CBHW071448160426
43195CB00013B/2053